CHILI LOVERS COOK BOOK

CHILI RECIPES
and RECIPES with CHILES

GOLDEN WEST ☼ PUBLISHERS

Chile or Chili?

The Spanish word "chile" is a variation of "chilli" from the Nahuatl dialect of the ancient Aztec Indians of Mexico.

As for "chili," its origin is obscure. Generally, though, "chili" is used principally to identify the tantalizing combination of meat and chile peppers, whose pungency ranges from mild to scorching.

A further complication is the employment of the term "chile con carne" which, literally translated from the Spanish, means "chile with meat." Traditionally, "chile con carne" is a dish which combines small pieces of meat simmered with chile peppers, served in stew-fashion, accompanied by tortillas.

Another seeming contradiction in the spelling controversy concerns the spelling of "chili powder." Although the powder is ground from red chile peppers, the product is labeled "chili powder."

Fortunately, the spelling strife disappears the moment a dish of chili appears!

Library of Congress Cataloging in Publication Data

Main entry under title:

Chili-lovers' Cook Book

Includes index.

1. Chili con carne.   2. Chili.   I. Fischer, Al

II. Fischer, Mildred

TX749.C48   641.8'2   78-16382

ISBN 0-914846-06-X

Printed in the United States of America

20th printing, ©1994

Golden West Publishers

4113 N. Longview Ave.

Phoenix, AZ 85014

(602) 265-4392

Contents

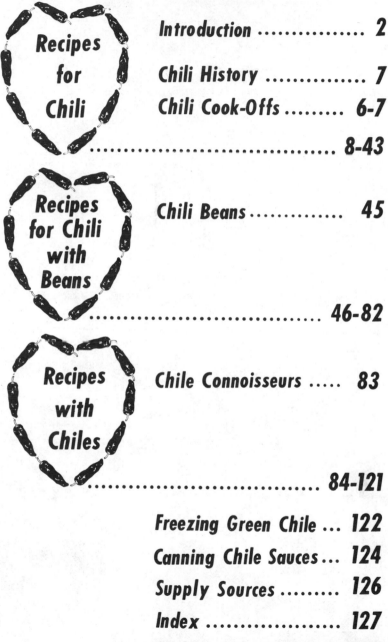

Chili mania focuses very simply on a bowl of chili. It is a craving, a passion, an obsession for a simmered combination of meat and chile peppers whose distinctive aroma makes an indelible imprint on the senses. Even the word "chili" is exciting to a chili-lover, for it evokes the memories of a dish that warms the heart and embraces the body in an aura of sensuous satisfaction. Chili is the ambrosia of modern man.

No one knows who made the first pot of chili. Much of the background information for the origin of chili is lost in antiquity or clouded by legend and romantic tales.

One of the most convincing stories revolves around chuck-wagon cooks who were accustomed to preparing their own brand of stew for the cowboys of the southwest. Possibly, one of these cooks ran out of the customary black pepper. In his search for a substitute, he came across some red peppers commonly in vogue among the Indians or Mexicans of the territory that is now southwest Texas. These peppers were violently hot, principally because they had not been domesticated by agricultural technologists. Likely enough, the cook employed the same quantity of red pepper that he had been using of black. When the cowboys complained about the intensity of the red pepper stew, they were advised that the heat of the dish was generated by the "chile"—a generic term which refers to hot peppers. As time passed, the searing stew was acknowledged as an entity in its own right, and "chili" was born.

Chili became so popular that chili parlors and chili cookoffs were a natural offshoot. A chili-cooking duel which began in jest between the late humorist H. Allen Smith and the late Texas journalist Wick Fowler in 1967 has mushroomed into a series of annual local and statewide competitions, culminating in major international contests.

Chili Cook-Offs

Chili-lovers can flock to the Wick Fowler Memorial Chili Cookoff at Terlingua, Texas, on the first Saturday and Sunday in November, an event sponsored by the Chili Appreciation Society International, or attend the World Championship Chili Cookoff, a one-day chili spectacular, sponsored by the International Chili Society (generally held in October at a California location which may change from year to year).

Now, try these long-treasured, often-secret chili dishes from chili masters!

Gila Chili

Vern McCandless -- Founder of Arizona Chili Society
Winner of the Western States Chili Cook-Off

SALAD OIL
5 lbs. CHUCK
1 can (8-oz.) TOMATO SAUCE
8 oz. WATER
2 cans (4-oz.) diced GREEN CHILES
8 tsp. Gebhardt's CHILI POWDER
1 tsp. PAPRIKA
1 tsp. Accent MSG
2 tsp. SALT
1 tsp. BLACK PEPPER
1 tsp. OREGANO (ground)
1 tsp. CUMIN SEEDS (roasted, crushed or ground)
1 cup warm WATER
1 cup ONIONS (chopped)
1 cup CELERY (chopped)
6 cloves GARLIC (chopped very fine)
1 tsp. TABASCO
3 tsp. Masa Harina (or regular flour)
1 cup warm WATER

(Use lean, rough-ground chuck or have meat cut into 1/4"
cubes.)

Put about 3 tablespoons oil in an iron (or aluminum) pot.
Add meat and sear until meat is gray. Add tomato sauce
PLUS 8-oz. of water to rinse out can. Add green chiles.

Combine chili powder, paprika, MSG, salt, black pepper,
oregano, cumin seeds and one cup of warm water in a pint
jar with tight lid. Shake well and add to meat mixture.

Heat salad oil in skillet and saute onions, celery, and garlic
until onions are clear. (DO NOT overcook). Add to meat and
cook for 2 1/2 hours. Add Tabasco and continue cooking.

Put Masa Harina (or regular flour) into the jar used for
spices. Add a cup of warm water and shake well; add to pot.
Rinse jar with water and add to pot.

After three hours of cooking, check for salt taste. (Optional:
add bay leaf for 30 minutes during cooking, then discard it. To
increase "hotness" of chili, increase Tabasco by teaspoons to
suit individual taste.) (Makes one gallon)

Wick Fowler's "Two Alarm" Chili

Congressman J. J. Pickle's version -- 10th District, Texas

3 lbs. MEAT (chili ground)
1 can (15-oz.) TOMATO SAUCE
1 ONION (chopped)
1 clove GARLIC (chopped)
1 tsp. SALT
1 tsp. CAYENNE
1 tsp. TABASCO
1 level Tbsp. OREGANO
1 level Tbsp. CUMIN
6 Red CHILI PEPPERS
    (optional)
4 heaping Tbsp. CHILI POWDER
1 level Tbsp. PAPRIKA
2 Tbsp. FLOUR
Water

Sear meat in skillet with onions and garlic. When meat is thoroughly seared, put in tomato sauce, add some water to cover meat. Add all other ingredients. Cover with half an inch of water and stir well. Simmer at least 1 1/2 hours (or longer), stirring regularly. Towards the end of cooking time, skim the grease; add flour mixed with warm water to thicken. (Serves 6)

Gebhardt's Chili con Carne

Courtesy Gebhardt's Mexican Foods -- San Antonio, Texas

2 lbs. MEAT (chopped fine)
4 Tbsp. Gebhardt's CHILI
    POWDER
2 cloves GARLIC (minced)
4 Tbsp. FLOUR
4 Tbsp. FAT
1 lg. ONION (chopped)
1 Tbsp. SALT
1 quart HOT WATER

Use cheaper cuts of meat; cut into small chunks (DO NOT grind). Mix with chili powder, garlic and flour. Melt fat in deep pot and saute onion until tender. Add the meat and cook 15 minutes. Add salt. Gradually pour on hot water. Simmer one hour (or until tender). (Serves 4 to 6)

Pedernales River Chili

Mrs. Lyndon B. Johnson -- Stonewall, Texas

4 lbs. CHILI MEAT*
1 lg. ONION (chopped)
2 cloves GARLIC
1 tsp. Ground OREGANO
1 tsp. COMINO SEED
6 tsp. CHILI POWDER
1½ cups canned Whole TOMATOES
2 to 6 generous dashes Liquid HOT SAUCE
SALT to taste
2 cups HOT WATER

(*Chili meat is coarsely ground round steak or well-trimmed chuck. If specially-ground, ask butcher to use 3/4" plate for coarse grind.)

Place meat, onion, garlic in large, heavy frypan or Dutch oven. Cook until light-colored. Add remaining ingredients. Bring to a boil, lower heat, simmer about an hour. Skim off fat during cooking. (Serves 10 to 12)

Ann's Texas Chili

Ann Burge -- Oglesby, Illinois

3 lbs. Boneless CHUCK (1" cubes)
2 Tbsp. Vegetable OIL
3 cloves GARLIC (chopped)
4 to 6 Tbsp. CHILI POWDER
2 tsp. ground CUMIN
3 Tbsp. FLOUR
1 Tbsp. leaf OREGANO
2 cans (13¾-oz.) BEEF BROTH
1 tsp. SALT
¼ tsp. PEPPER

Heat oil in a 4-quart pot, add beef, stirring frequently until meat loses color. (DO NOT brown). Lower heat, stir in garlic. Combine chili powder, cumin and flour. Sprinkle meat with chili mixture, stirring until meat is evenly coated. Crumble oregano over meat. Add 1 1/2 cans broth and stir til liquid is well blended. Add salt and pepper. Bring to a boil, stirring occasionally. Reduce heat; simmer partially covered over low heat for 1 1/2 hours. Stir occasionally.

Add remaining broth, cook 30 minutes more. Cool thoroughly. Cover and refrigerate overnight. Reheat chili in top part of double boiler placed over boiling water. (Serves 8)

Stella Hughes' Chili con Carne

Stella Hughes -- Author of CHUCK WAGON COOKIN'

2 Tbsp. BACON FRYINGS
2 lbs. lean BEEF (chuck or rump)
1 lg. ONION (chopped fine)
2 cloves GARLIC (diced fine)
1 can (#2½) TOMATOES (diced)
½ cup El Pato RED CHILI SAUCE (OR enchilada sauce)
1 heaping Tbsp. Santa Cruz RED CHILI POWDER
½ tsp. OREGANO
1 tsp. Accent MSG
½ cup VINEGAR
1 rounded Tbsp. BROWN SUGAR
SALT and PEPPER to taste
WATER

Cut meat into bite-size pieces. (DO NOT use hamburger.) Brown meat in a heavy iron skillet or Dutch oven in bacon fryings (or lard). When beef is nicely browned, add onions and garlic. Continue cooking until onions are about half done, then add remaining ingredients.

Cook over low heat until meat is very tender. Let cook down and add hot water, a little at a time to keep from sticking. Do not add thickening. (Serves 6)

Honest-to-God Chili

Courtesy Carroll Shelby's Original Texas Brand Chili Preparation

2 lb. lean BEEF (coarse ground)
1 can (8-oz.) TOMATO SAUCE
1 can (8-oz.) WATER
1 pkg. Carroll Shelby's TEXAS BRAND CHILI

Grind the meat coarse (or cut it into chunks the size of half your little toe). Sear the meat until it's good and brown. Dump the meat into a chili pot and add tomato sauce and water. Simmer for 15 minutes. Add Texas Chili spice packet. Bring mixture to a boil, then simmer for at least half an hour. Stir carefully to prevent sticking. Keep lid on as much as possible to keep the "pot likker" inside. Add water as needed.

Mix packet of masa flour with water to form watery paste and stir in slowly. (At this point, you can add pepper pods, canned or cooked chili, or beans to suit personal taste.) Simmer another 15 or 20 minutes. (Serves 6)

Jay's Chili

Jay Pennington -- Las Vegas, Nevada
World Champion at Tropico Gold Mine, Calif.,Chili Cookoff

1 Tbsp. cooking OIL
3 med. ONIONS
2 BELL PEPPERS
2 CELERY STALKS
3 GARLIC CLOVES
8 lbs. coarse-ground ROUND
   STEAK (lean chili grind)
2 cans (#2) Contadina TOMATO SAUCE
2 cans (#2) Contadina STEWED TOMATOES
2 cans (#2) WATER
1 can (6-oz.) Contadina TOMATO PASTE
1 can (4-oz.) CHILI SALSA
1 green HOT CHILI PEPPER (3")
   (only 1 chili from can) chopped fine
2 bottles (3-oz. ea.) CHILI POWDER
1 can (4-oz.) GREEN CHILI (diced)
Dash of OREGANO
SALT (approx. 3 Tbsp.)
PEPPER (coarse ground)
GARLIC SALT

Put oil in a 10 to 12 qt. pot. Add onions, peppers, celery and garlic cloves. Cook until onion is transparent. Add meat slowly, and stir until redness disappears. Add remaining ingredients, stirring after each addition. Lower heat to simmer, and simmer for 2 1/2 to 3 hours. Stir to prevent scorching. (Serves 12 to 16)

Goldie's Good Chili

Goldie (Mrs. Jack) Gomez -- Hobbs, New Mexico

4 lbs. FLANK STEAK
2 lbs. PORK CHOPS (center cut)
1 tsp. CUMIN SEEDS
1 tsp. OREGANO
3 cups ONIONS (chopped)
½ cup CELERY (chopped)
4 med. TOMATOES (Chopped)

2 Tbsp. OIL
4 cans (7-oz.) CHILE SALSA
4 cups GREEN CHILES (chopped)
3 Tbsp. CHILI POWDER
1 Tbsp. PAPRIKA
2 cloves GARLIC (crushed)
1 quart WATER
2½ tsp. SALT

Grind flank steak and pork separately (or cube). Cook meats separately until gray in color. Add cumin and oregano and cook 1/2 hour, uncovered. Stir often. In separate saucepan, cook onions and celery in oil. Add onions to meat mixture and stir. Then add remaining ingredients and simmer 60 minutes more. (Makes 1 1/2 gallons)

Reno Red Championship Chili

Joe and Shirley Stewart— California

1979 World Champions at Tropico Gold Mine, Calif.,
Chili Cookoff

3 lbs. ROUND STEAK (coarse ground)
3 lbs. CHUCK STEAK (coarse ground)
1 cup Wesson OIL (or Kidney Suet)
Black PEPPER to taste
1 bottle (3 oz.) Gebhardt CHILI POWDER
6 Tbsp. CUMIN
2 Tbsp. MSG
6 small cloves GARLIC (minced)
2 ONIONS (medium) chopped
6 Dried CHILI PODS (Remove stems and seeds
    and boil 30 minutes in water.) OR 3 oz. New
    Mexico Chili Pepper
1 Tbsp. OREGANO (brewed in ½ cup Budweiser
    Beer, like tea)
2 Tbsp. PAPRIKA
2 Tbsp. CIDER VINEGAR
3 cups BEEF BROTH
1 can (4 oz.) Ortega GREEN CHILI (diced)
½ can (14½ oz.) Hunt's STEWED TOMATOES
    (or to taste)
1 tsp. TABASCO (or to taste)
2 Tbsp. MASA FLOUR

Brown meat in oil (or suet), adding black pepper to taste. Drain meat and add chili powder, cumin, MSG, garlic and chopped onions. Cook 30-35 minutes, using as little liquid as possible. Add water only as necessary. Stir often.

Remove skins from boiled chili pods. Mash pulp and add to meat mixture (or add chili pepper), strained oregano and beer mixture, paprika, vinegar, two (2) cups beef broth, diced green chili, stewed tomatoes and Tabasco sauce. Simmer 30-45 minutes, stirring often.

Dissolve Masa flour into remaining beef broth and pour into chili. Simmer 30 minutes more, stirring often. Serves 12-15.

(It's important to keep the chili thick during cooking, so that it's almost dry. If too much water is added, the spices will be soaked off the meat, and no amount of cooking to reduce the liquid will correct this.)

Capitol Punishment Chili

William Pfeiffer— Arlington, Va.

1980 World Champion at International Chili Society Cookoff

1 Tbsp. OREGANO
2 Tbsp. PAPRIKA
2 Tbsp. MSG
9 Tbsp. (rounded, almost heaping) CHILI
  POWDER (Light)
4 Tbsp. (heaping) CUMIN
4 Tbsp. BEEF BOUILLON (Instant crushed)
1 can Budweiser BEER
1 cup WATER
4 lbs. extra lean CHUCK (chili ground)
2 lbs. extra lean PORK (chili ground)
1 lb. extra lean CHUCK (cut in ¼ cubes)
½ cup Wesson OIL (or Kidney Suet)
2 large ONIONS (chopped fine)
10 cloves GARLIC (chopped fine)
1 tsp. MOLE (powdered)
1 Tbsp. SUGAR
1 tsp. CORIANDER
1 tsp. Louisiana RED HOT! SAUCE (Durkee)
6 oz. Hunt's TOMATO SAUCE
1 Tbsp. Masa Harina FLOUR
SALT to taste

In a large pot, add oregano, paprika, MSG, chili powder, cumin, beef bouillon, beer and water. Let simmer.

In a separate skillet, brown 1½ pounds meat with one tablespoon oil (or suet) until meat is light brown. Drain and add to simmering spices. Continue browning process until all meat has been added to spices.

Saute onions and garlic in one tablespoon oil (or suet). Add to spices and meat mixture. (Mixture should be thick enough so that a spoon would stand in it. For thinner mixture, add beer or water at personal discretion.) Simmer two hours.

Add mole, sugar, coriander, hot sauce, tomato sauce and simmer another 45 minutes.

Dissolve flour in warm water (pasty mixture) and add to chili. Add salt to taste. Simmer 30 minutes longer. (For hotter chili, add additional hot sauce.) (Serves 12 to 15)

The Chairman's
Champeen Chili, Okie Style

Dewey Mattox, Pres. Arizona Chili Society -- Avondale, Arizona

6 lbs. BEEF (special coarse chili
   ground)
2 lbs. PORK (coarse ground)
2 oz. PAPRIKA
4 lg. ONIONS (chopped)
1 clove GARLIC (minced)
3 cans (16-oz.) Whole TOMATOES

½ tsp. BLACK PEPPER
1 tsp. SAVOR SALT
2 oz. CHILI POWDER
½ tsp. OREGANO
1 oz. CUMIN
3 JALAPENO PEPPERS (chopped)

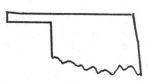

Brown meat with paprika. Drain fat and saute onions and garlic in separate pan. Combine with meat and add remaining ingredients. Cook slowly over low heat for three hours. (Serves 8 to 10)

Harmon's Chili

Harmon V. Averyt -- Yuma, Arizona

½ cup cooking OIL
3 med. ONIONS (chopped)
3 cloves GARLIC (chopped)
3 lbs. HAMBURGER (coarse ground)
1 can (16-oz.) TOMATOES (mashed)
1 can (8-oz.) TOMATO SAUCE
4 Tbsp. New Mexico GROUND CHILI
1 Tbsp. OREGANO POWDER
1 tsp. CUMIN POWDER
1 Tbsp. SALT
½ tsp. BLACK PEPPER
1 tsp. CAYENNE POWDER
1 quart WATER

Heat oil and saute onions and garlic until almost brown. Add ground meat and cook until redness is done (but don't burn meat). Add tomatoes, tomato sauce and all seasonings. Stir thoroughly. Add water to thin, if needed. Simmer for about an hour. Stir often to prevent burning. (Serves 6 to 8)

Wood's Undenia-Bull World Championship Chili

C. V. Wood, Jr. -- Los Angeles, California
Undefeated World Chili Champion

3-lb. STEWING CHICKEN or
  4 cans (10-oz.) Chicken Broth
1½ quarts WATER
½ lb. Beef Kidney SUET (or 4-oz. oil)
4 lbs. FLANK STEAK
5 lbs. PORK CHOPS (thin, center cut)
¼ cup CELERY
6 lg. ripe TOMATOES
2 tsp. SUGAR
6 GREEN CHILES (Anaheim Green or New Mexico #6)
8-oz. light BEER

3 tsp. OREGANO (ground)
3 tsp. CUMIN (ground)
3 tsp. BLACK PEPPER (fine)
4 tsp. SALT
5 Tbsp. CHILI POWDER (use unblended powder)
1 tsp. CILANTRO
1 tsp. THYME
½ tsp. MSG
3 med. ONIONS
2 GREEN PEPPERS
2 cloves GARLIC
1 lb. JACK Cheese (grated)
1 lg. LIME

For this recipe, you'll need a two-gallon cooking pot, a two-quart saucepan, a large skillet, a wire (or plastic strainer), and a wooden spoon.

Step #1--cut stewing chicken into pieces. In two-gallon pot, combine cut-up chicken and water; simmer for two hours. (Reserve cooked chicken for other dishes.)

Step #2--While chicken cooks, render suet to make 6 to 8 tablespoons oil. Discard fat and keep the oil.

Step #3--Trim all fat off flank steak; dice into 3/8" cubes.

Step #4--Trim all fat and bones off pork chops; dice into 1/4" cubes.

Step #5--In two-quart saucepan put celery (chopped very fine), peeled and chopped tomatoes and sugar. Simmer about 1 1/2 hours until ingredients are completely tender.

Step #6--Blister green chiles, remove skins, and boil for 15 minutes until tender. Remove seeds and cut into 1/4" squares.

Step #7--Put oregano, cumin, black pepper, salt, chili powder, cilantro, thyme and MSG into beer and stir until all lumps dissolve.

Step #8--Chop onions into 1/4" pieces (two cups); chop peppers into 3/8" pieces (two cups). Chop garlic very fine.

Step #9--To the chicken broth in the two-gallon pot, add the celery-tomato mixture, the cut chilis, the spices and beer mixture, and the chopped garlic. Stir with wooden spoon and bring to a low simmer.

Step #10--Brown pork in skillet with 1/3 oil from Step #2. (Brown only one-half pork cubes at a time. Pork should become

white on all sides and fully separate. DO NOT overcook pork.)
Step #11--Add browned pork to chicken broth and bring to a
low boil for about 30 minutes.
Step #12--With balance of oil, brown beef (about 1/3 at a time).
Beef should get white on all sides. DO NOT OVERCOOK.
Step #13--Add beef to chicken broth and cook at a low boil
for about an hour.
Step #14--Add chopped onions and peppers.
Step #15--Cook over low boil for about two to three hours,
stirring with wooden spoon every 15 or 20 minutes.

Step #16--Remove chili from stove and allow to cool for an
hour. Refrigerate 24 hours for spices to permeate. Chili can
be reheated (or frozen) after 24 hours. (If reheating, use
1/6th pound grated Jack cheese to each quart of chili, add,
and stir with wooden spoon until completely dissolved.) About
a minute before serving, add juice of lime and stir with wooden
spoon. (Makes 6 quarts)

Chili Salinas

Wanda Livingston -- Salinas, California

2 Tbsp. OLIVE OIL
2 med. ONIONS (chopped fine)
2 or 3 cloves GARLIC (crushed)
3 lbs. CHUCK (coarse ground)
½ cup BELL PEPPER (chopped)
½ cup CELERY (chopped)
1 can (4-oz.) GREEN CHILES
   (diced)
1 can (#2) stewed TOMATOES
   (chopped)
1 can (#2) TOMATO SAUCE
1 bottle (2-oz.) CHILI POWDER
½ tsp. OREGANO (not powdered)
1 tsp. CUMIN
2 tsp. SALT
Sprinkling Fresh Ground Pepper

Place oil, onions and garlic in large pot and saute over
medium heat for one minute. Add meat to pot and cook over
medium heat until redness disappears. (DO NOT brown). Add
remaining ingredients in order given, and bring to boil. Turn
heat to low, cover pot, and simmer for at least three hours.
Stir to prevent sticking. (If too much liquid cooks out, add
small amounts of hot beef bouillon--about 1/2 cup at a time.
Chili should be thick.)(Serves 6)

Lawry's Authentic Texas-Style Chili

Courtesy Lawry's Foods, Inc. -- Los Angeles, California

2 lbs. CHILI MEAT
Lawry's Texas Style CHILI Seasoning MIX
1 can (8-oz.) TOMATO SAUCE
2 cups WATER

In a 5-quart Dutch oven, brown the chili meat. (Or use 2 1/4 pounds chuck steak, cut into 1/4" cubes OR use 2 pounds lean ground beef.) Drain fat. Add the chili mix, tomato sauce and water. Blend well. Bring to a boil, reduce heat and simmer slowly, covered, for 45 to 60 minutes. Stir occasionally. (Makes 5 cups)

Chili por J. I. Gardner

J. I. Gardner -- Lakeside, Arizona
Champion, Arizona Magazine Chili Burn-Off

5 lbs. BEEF CHUCK (Elk or Venison)
2 lbs. PORK SHOULDER
1 lg. ONION
6 med. cloves GARLIC
12 to 16 Dried RED CHILES
1 Tbsp. OREGANO
1 tsp. CUMIN
1 tsp. BLACK PEPPER
SALT to taste

Trim all fat, gristle and bone from meat and cut into half-inch cubes. Cut all usable fat into small cubes and render until fat is brown. Lift out rendered fat pieces and save the grease for frying cubed meat. Saute meat until it leaves the red stage. (DO NOT overfry.)

Wash red chili pods and remove stems and seeds. Soak chilis in hot water for 20 to 30 minutes. Pour water from chiles into blender, and add chiles a few at a time. Blend until a creamy consistency.

Peel onion and garlic. Cut into small pieces and put into blender with enough oil to start onions and garlic to blend. Blend until creamy. Place in frypan and saute until lemon-colored.

Put all ingredients into two-gallon pot, and simmer until meat is tender. Skim off excess oil and thicken with a thickening of flour (or corn starch) to desired consistency. To add more "bite" add a small amount of cayenne. (Makes one gallon)

Roundup Chili

Steven A. Hotch -- San Bernardino, California

3 dry mild Red CHILI PEPPERS
4 cups WATER
4 lbs. GROUND BEEF
1 lg. ONION (chopped fine)
3 cloves GARLIC (chopped fine)
3 stalks CELERY (chopped fine)
1 can (8-oz.) TOMATO SAUCE
1 can (4-oz.) diced GREEN CHILES
1 Tbsp. CUMIN (ground)
1 Tbsp. Whole OREGANO
1 whole BAY LEAF
3 Tbsp. mild CHILI POWDER
¼ tsp. RED PEPPER FLAKES
¼ tsp. WHITE PEPPER
½ tsp. BLACK PEPPER
1 tsp. PAPRIKA
1 Beef BOUILLON Cube
½ sq. Unsweetened CHOCOLATE
1 Tbsp. FLOUR
3 Tbsp. CORN MEAL
SALT to taste

Soak poppers in water. When soft, remove from water (save water). Grind peppers fine in meat grinder or food processor. Brown meat and drain off extra fat. Add onion and garlic to meat; cook for five minutes, stirring occasionally. Add celery, tomato sauce, green chiles, cumin, oregano, bay leaf, chili powder, red pepper flakes, white and black pepper, paprika, bouillon cube, ground chile peppers PLUS the water used to soak chile peppers. Bring to a boil, cover, reduce the heat and simmer for one hour, stirring occasionally.

Add chocolate and stir until completely melted. Cover and simmer very slowly for 1/2 hour, stirring occasionally. Mix flour and corn meal together. Add enough water to make a thin paste. Stir into meat mixture; cook, uncovered, for five minutes, stirring constantly, until slightly thickened. Add salt to taste. Remove bay leaf. (Serves 8)

This recipe is best when made in a well-seasoned iron pot, but any pot can be used. It freezes very well. Store in freezer in small aluminum pans -- one cup per pan -- or in well-washed milk cartons.

Diane's Crockpot Chili

Diane Deiber -- Santa Cruz, California

8 lbs. BEEF (coarse ground)
3 ONIONS (medium)
2 BELL PEPPERS
3 CELERY STALKS
1 can (6-oz.) TOMATO PASTE
2 cans (16-oz.) stewed TOMATOES
2 cans (#2) TOMATO SAUCE
3 GARLIC CLOVES (chopped)
2 bottles (3-oz.) CHILI POWDER
3 Tbsp. SALT
1 can (1-oz.) CHILE SALSA
1 tsp. GREEN HOT CHILI
  (canned, diced)
GARLIC SALT
Coarse ground PEPPER
OREGANO

Brown ground beef in frying pan. Pour off extra fat. Put browned meat in crock pot (3 1/2 or 5 quart size). Chop the onions, peppers and celery stalks fine. Add chopped vegetables and all other ingredients to crock pot. Cook on low heat for three hours. (Serves 16)

Lemon-Wine Chili

Mary A. Frye -- Sacramento, California

1 lb. ground BEEF (lean)
1 med. ONION (chopped fine)
1 clove GARLIC (minced fine)
1 can (28-oz.) stewed TOMATOES
1 cup BURGUNDY WINE
JUICE of lg. fresh LEMON
4 Tbsp. CHILI POWDER
1 tsp. SEASONED SALT
½ tsp. LEMON PEPPER
¼ tsp. BLACK PEPPER (seasoned)
¼ tsp. CAYENNE PEPPER
½ tsp. hot DRY MUSTARD
½ tsp. CELERY SEED
½ tsp. CUMIN
¼ tsp. OREGANO

Brown beef with onions and garlic, stirring frequently. Add remaining ingredients and simmer for at least one hour. (Serves 6)

Nevada Annie's Championship Chili

LaVerne Harris -- Las Vegas, Nevada
World Champion at Tropico Gold Mine,Calif.,Chili Cookoff

3 Tbsp. Wesson OIL
1½ med. ONIONS (chopped)
1 med. GREEN PEPPER
  chopped)
1 lg. rib CELERY (chopped)
1 sm. clove GARLIC (minced)
½ tsp. fresh JALAPENO
  PEPPER (chopped)
4 lbs. GROUND ROUND
  (coarse)
8 Tbsp. CHILI POWDER
1 Tbsp. CUMIN (ground)
2 tsp. GARLIC SALT

¼ tsp. TABASCO Pepper
  Sauce
SALT & PEPPER
8-oz. Budweiser BEER
1¼ cups WATER
1 can (14½-oz.) Hunts Stewed
  TOMATOES
1 can (8-oz.) Hunt's TOMATO
  SAUCE
1 can (6-oz.) Hunt's TOMATO
  PASTE
1 can (4-oz.) Ortega diced
  GREEN CHILES
1 BAY LEAF

Heat oil and saute first five ingredients until onion is transparent. Add beef and cook until meat loses its redness. Combine chili powder, cumin, garlic salt, Tabasco sauce, salt and pepper with beer. Let mixture stand 1 to 2 minutes. Then add beer and spice mix, water, stewed tomatoes, tomato sauce, tomato paste, green chiles, and bay leaf to meat mixture. Simmer on low heat in a covered pot for three hours, stirring often. Remove bay leaf before serving. (Makes 10 servings.)

Don's "Hot-Damn" Chili

Donald W. Coleman -- Mesa, Arizona
Arizona State Chili Champion

3 lbs. ROUND STEAK
  (cubed)
1 lb. PORK STEAK (cubed)
2 lg. ONIONS (diced)
3 cans (14½-oz.) whole
  TOMATOES
6 Tbsp. CHILI POWDER
1 Tbsp. CUMIN (ground)

1 Tbsp. OREGANO (ground)
2 Tbsp. SALT
2 Tbsp. CAYENNE
5 lg. GARLIC CLOVES
  (minced)
WATER
5 Tbsp. Yellow
  CORNMEAL

Cook meat in own juices until redness is gone. Add onions, tomatoes, spices (cumin seed and oregano must be freshly ground), and garlic. Add water to suit desired consistency. Cook two hours over medium heat in pressure cooker with cover, but WITHOUT pressure lid. Add corn meal and cook for one additional hour (or until meat is tender). Makes 5 quarts of chili.

Butterfield Stage Line Chili

Fred Drexel—Van Nuys, California
1981 World Champion at International Chili Society Cookoff

1 can (8-oz.) Budweiser BEER
½ oz. TEQUILA
2 cans (8-oz. each) Hunts TOMATO SAUCE
1 cube Wylers BEEF BOUILLON
2½ cups WATER
5 cloves GARLIC (minced fine)
½ can (7-oz.) Ortega CHILES
13 Tbsp. Gebhardts CHILI POWDER
5 Tbsp. ground CUMIN
¼ tsp. DRY MUSTARD
¼ tsp. MSG
1½ tsp. BROWN SUGAR
Pinch OREGANO
4 Tbsp. Wesson OIL
5 lbs. BEEF BRISKET (cubed small)
1 lb. LEAN PORK (fresh ground)
2 large ONIONS (chopped fine)
SALT & PEPPER

In a large covered pot (preferably an iron one, or a crockpot) simmer the beer, tequila, tomato sauce, beef bouillon cube, water, garlic, chiles, chili powder, cumin, dry mustard, MSG, brown sugar and oregano.

In a separate pan, brown the beef, pork and onions in oil. Add salt and pepper to taste. Add the meat and onions to other pot.

Cover and simmer for at least three hours, stirring frequently. (Serves 8 to 10)

Venison Chili

Mrs. Clyde Gilbreth -- Paducah, Texas

2 Tbsp. vegetable OIL
1 lb. VENISON chili meat
1 small ONION (grated)
1 small GARLIC BUD (grated)
1 tsp. SALT
1 dash CAYENNE pepper
3 Tbsp. Mexicana CHILI POWDER
½ tsp. OREGANO
3 cups HOT WATER

Heat oil in large utensil. Add meat and fry until brown. Add onion and garlic and saute lightly. When onions are transparent, add salt, pepper, chili powder and oegano. Stir. Add hot water, cover and bring to a boil. Lower heat and simmer 30 minutes (or until meat is tender). (Serves 6 to 8)

Bob Moore's Championship Chili Recipe

Bob Moore— Spring, Texas
1980 World Champion, Arriba Terlingua, Texas

5 lbs. boneless SIRLOIN TIP ROAST (remove
all visible fat and connecting tissue. Hand
cut into ⅜" cubes)
4 Tbsp. KIDNEY FAT (minced)
2 medium WHITE ONIONS (minced)
1 can (12 oz.) LONE STAR BEER
1 can (8 oz.) TOMATO SAUCE
1 can (8 oz.) HOT WATER
1 can (12 oz.) BEEF STOCK
6 large GARLIC PODS (mashed in 1 Tbsp. oil.
Mash until puree is formed)
5 Tbsp. PAPRIKA (Mexican)
2 tsp. SALT
1 Tbsp. FLAVOR ENHANCER
1½ tsp. PEPPER
11 Tbsp. CHILI POWDER, Unblended (Mexican)
5½ Tbsp. CUMIN (fine grind, Mexican)
1 tsp. OREGANO
¼ tsp. Ground CHILE JAPONES (or Chile Arbol
—for additional heat)

In a frying pan, brown the meat with rendered kidney fat until gray in color. (Brown about two pounds at a time with a tablespoon of rendered kidney fat.) Return meat and natural juices to cooking pot. Saute onions in a tablespoon of rendered kidney fat until translucent. Return to pot.

Add beer, tomato sauce, hot water, beef stock, ½ mashed garlic mixture, two tablespoons paprika, one teaspoon salt, one tablespoon flavor enhancer and one teaspoon pepper.

Simmer (covered) over low heat for two hours until meat is tender. Be sure pot has a tight lid, as this will help the tenderizing process. Stir occasionally.

When meat is tender, add remainder of garlic mixture, unblended chili powder, cumin, three tablespoons paprika, oregano, one teaspoon salt, ½ teaspoon pepper, chiles, and continue cooking for 15 more minutes. Turn heat off and let set for one or two hours, so that the flavor of the spices is absorbed. After one or two hours of rest, turn heat back on and continue to simmer for one additional hour. Total cooking time is 3 hours, 15 minutes. (Serves 10)

George House Chili

Carol George -- Northridge, California

3½ lbs TOP ROUND
5 Tbsp. OIL
2 cups ONION (chopped coarse)
4 cloves GARLIC (minced)
4 Tbsp. CHILI POWDER
1½ tsp. OREGANO
1½ tsp. ground CUMIN

1 tsp. crushed RED PEPPER
2 cups BEEF BROTH
1 can (29-oz.) TOMATOES
1 can (6-oz.) TOMATO PASTE
1 Tbsp. SALT
1 tsp. SUGAR
1 to 2 Tbsp. yellow CORN MEAL

Cut meat into 1/2" cubes and pat dry. Heat 3 tablespoons oil in large, heavy pot. When pot is hot, add meat all at once. Sear, turning constantly, until all pieces are lightly browned (about 3 or 4 minutes).

Using slotted spoon, transfer meat to a bowl. Add remaining 2 tablespoons oil to pot. Add onion and garlic and saute until golden. Stir in chili powder, oregano, cumin, and crushed red pepper. Mix well until onions are coated. Add broth, tomatoes (with juice), tomato paste, salt and sugar, and mix well. Break up tomatoes with back of spoon.

Put meat back in pot, cover, bring to a boil. Then simmer for one hour. Uncover, simmer for 40 to 50 minutes (until meat is very tender. Cool, cover and refrigerate overnight.

To serve, bring slowly to a boil, simmer until heated through-out. (If chili is too liquid, simmer uncovered. Otherwise, heat covered. Thicken with cornmeal, if necessary.) (Serves 8)

Maria's Best

Mary Jo Marshall -- Tucson, Arizona

2 cups WATER
1 lb. CHILI BRICK (frozen)
1 lb. GROUND BEEF
1 clove GARLIC (crushed)
2 lg. ONIONS (chopped)
1 lg. GREEN PEPPER (chopped)
2 small cans TOMATO PUREE
1 Tbsp. CHILI POWDER
½ tsp. CUMIN
SALT and PEPPER to taste

In large saucepan, heat water and chili brick, which has been broken into pieces with a fork. Heat until mixed well and set aside. Brown crumbled ground beef in skillet. Add remaining ingredients and stir thoroughly as mixture heats. Add beef mixture to saucepan containing chili brick. Mix thoroughly and simmer one hour, stirring occasionally. (Serves 4 to 6)

West Texas Chili

Lynda (Mrs. Jim) Grimsley -- Friona, Texas

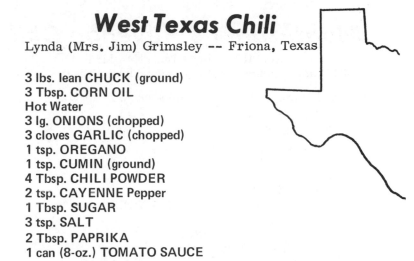

3 lbs. lean CHUCK (ground)
3 Tbsp. CORN OIL
Hot Water
3 lg. ONIONS (chopped)
3 cloves GARLIC (chopped)
1 tsp. OREGANO
1 tsp. CUMIN (ground)
4 Tbsp. CHILI POWDER
2 tsp. CAYENNE Pepper
1 Tbsp. SUGAR
3 tsp. SALT
2 Tbsp. PAPRIKA
1 can (8-oz.) TOMATO SAUCE
3 Tbsp. MASA HARINA

Put meat into large, cast-iron pot. Add corn oil to meat and sear over high heat, stirring constantly until meat turns light gray. Add hot water to just cover meat. Then add remaining ingredients EXCEPT masa flour, and simmer 2 1/2 hours. Dip off all grease. (If chili is too thin, sprinkle with masa flour and stir for 15 more minutes.) (Serves 6 to 8)

Mucker's Chili

Robert Hall -- Henderson, Nevada

1 Tbsp. OIL
1 lb. ground MEAT (lean)
½ tsp. Accent
1/8 tsp. GARLIC POWDER or
    1 clove GARLIC (cut fine)
1 Tbsp. SOY SAUCE
2 Tbsp. CHILI POWDER
½ tsp. CUMIN
¼ tsp. ground OREGANO
¼ cup ONION (chopped)
1 Tbsp. CORN FLOUR
½ cup TOMATO SAUCE or
    Chili Sauce
1 cup WATER

Heat oil in frying pan. Combine all seasonings and chopped onion with meat and brown mixture in heated pan. Add corn flour to browned meat and mix well. Add tomato (or chili sauce) and water. Bring to a boil, then simmer until done. (Serves 2)

Montezuma's Revenge Chili

Harold R. Timber—Taos, New Mexico
1983 World Champion at International Chili Society Cookoff

In a small saucepan dissolve the following in 2 cups water:

1 Tbsp. SUGAR
8 oz. BEEF CONSOMME
2 tsp. OREGANO
2 Tbsp. PAPRIKA
2 Tbsp. CUMIN
1 Tbsp. CELERY SALT
7 Tbsp. Gebhardts CHILI POWDER
2 Tbsp. MSG
1 tsp. CAYENNE PEPPER
1 tsp. GARLIC POWDER
1 Tbsp. MOLE (paste)

When this is dissolved, add this mixture to a 6-quart cooking pot, and keep at a light boil.

In a frying pan saute the following ingredients in a little Wesson Oil:

2 lbs. BEEF CHUCK (cut by hand in ⅜" cubes)
2 lbs. TOP ROUND of BEEF (coarsely ground)
2 lbs. PORK BUTT (medium ground)

Add the meat to the 6-quart cookpot.
Saute the following ingredients in a little Wesson Oil:

3 cups ONION (finely minced)
2 Tbsp. fresh GARLIC (finely minced)

Add mixture to 6-quart cookpot, along with the following:

1 cup GREEN CHILES (chopped)

Then add:

1 can (20-oz.) Hunt's TOMATO SAUCE

Bring the pot to a boil and add:

1 can Old Milwaukee BEER

Simmer uncovered for about 1½ to 2 hours, stirring occasionally. Let stand for ½ hour and skim off excess grease. Correct seasoning to taste. Thicken with Masa Harina in warm water to suitable consistency. Cover and let stand one hour before serving.

Mr. McIlhenny's Chili

Courtesy McIlhenny Co., mfrs. TABASCO Brand Pepper Sauce

3 lbs. lean STEW BEEF (1" cubes, well trimmed)
¼ cup SALAD OIL
1 cup ONION (chopped)
3 cloves GARLIC (minced)
4 to 6 Tbsp. CHILI POWDER
2 tsp. SALT
2 tsp. ground CUMIN
2 tsp. TABASCO Pepper Sauce
1 can (4-oz.) GREEN CHILES (seeded and chopped)
1 quart WATER
¼ cup ONIONS (chopped)

In large saucepan, brown beef in oil. Add remaining ingredients and mix well. Bring to a boil, reduce heat and simmer uncovered 1 1/2 to 2 hours (until meat is tender). Garnish with chopped onion and serve with a bottle of Tabasco sauce on the side. (Serves 4 to 6)

Goodwin's Gringo Chili con Carne

Arthur L. Goodwin, Jr. -- Mesa, Arizona

1 lg. jar whole MUSHROOMS
3 lg. GREEN PEPPERS
3 lbs. Top ROUND
6 Tbsp. Vegetable OIL
2 cups ONION (chopped coarse)
2 Tbsp. GARLIC POWDER
4 Tbsp. CHILI POWDER
1 tsp. OREGANO
1 tsp. ground CUMIN
1 tsp. RED PEPPER FLAKES
1 can (6-oz.) TOMATO PASTE
4 cups BEEF STOCK (fresh or canned)
1 tsp. SALT
Fresh Ground BLACK PEPPER

Heat one tablespoon vegetable oil in a 12-inch heavy skillet. Slice mushrooms lengthwise, chop green peppers into small bits. Add mushrooms and peppers to skillet; stir together five minutes. With slotted spoon, transfer mushrooms and peppers to a 4-quart heavy pot.

Pat meat dry with paper towels. Heat 4 tablespoons oil in skillet until light haze forms. Add meat and sear over high heat for three minutes, stirring, until meat is lightly browned. (For convenience, brown one pound of meat at one time.) Add meat to 4-quart pot.

Add remaining tablespoon of oil to skillet and cook onion and garlic powder for five minutes, stirring frequently. Remove skillet from heat, add chili powder, oregano, cumin, pepper flakes and stir until onions are well coated. Add tomato paste and stir again, until onions are well coated. Add coated onions to meat pot, then pour in beef stock. Mix ingredients thoroughly. Add salt and few grindings of black pepper.

Bring mixture to a boil, stirring once or twice, then half cover the pot, turn heat to low and simmer for 1 1/2 hours. (Serves 6 to 8)

Bildors Chili

Wilmer E. Dike -- Fillmore, California

2 Tbsp. Planters PEANUT OIL
1½ lbs. BELL PEPPERS (chopped)
1¼ lbs. ONIONS (chopped)
2 cans (28-oz.) crushed TOMATOES
1 can (12-oz.) TOMATO PASTE
3½ lbs. O-Bone ROAST (coarse grind)
1 cube BUTTER
¼ tsp. powdered GARLIC
½ cup PARSLEY (chopped)
¼ cup CHILI POWDER
2 Tbsp. SALT
3 tsp. powdered CUMIN
1½ tsp. BLACK PEPPER
1½ tsp. MSG
1 tsp. CAYENNE Red Pepper
½ can BACO-BITS

Saute bell peppers in oil for five minutes. Add onions and cook until tender. Add tomatoes and tomato paste (use 1/2 cup water to rinse tomato cans) to onion-pepper mixture and simmer five minutes.

In a separate pan, saute ground meat in butter for fifteen minutes (until brown). Add garlic, parsley and chili powder and cook five minutes more.

Add meat to onion-tomato mixture; then stir in all other spices. Stir well and simmer, covered, for one hour. Add water if necessary, and stir often. Simmer, uncovered, for thirty more minutes.

Use 1/2 cup water to add to chili mixture, if necessary. Add Baco-Bits and simmer ten minutes more. Serve hot over hot, cooked rice or hot, cooked pinto beans. (Serves 15)

Tommie Vanover's Chili

Tommie Vanover -- Chili Champion, Phoenix, Arizona

SUET (or ¼ cup Oil)
2 cups BEEF (ground)
SALT and PEPPER
2 lg. Red CHILE PEPPERS
 (peeled and chopped)
1 med. ONION (chopped)
BROTH (or water)
1 clove GARLIC
2 tsp. Whole COMINO
2 or 3 CHILETEPINS

Heat suet and brown beef. Add salt and pepper. Add onion, chopped chili peppers and enough broth (or water) to cover. Tie garlic, comino and chiletepins in a cheesecloth bag. Add spice bag to boiling beef and simmer until tender. Remove bag and thicken slightly with flour and water. (Serves 6)

New Mexico Chili

United States Senator Pete V. Domenici -- New Mexico

1 lb. PORK (cubed)
1 lb. BEEF (cubed)
2 cans (4-oz.) GREEN CHILES
   (diced)
1 clove GARLIC (diced)
Salt and Pepper

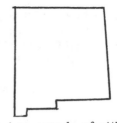

(In place of beef-pork combination, use two pounds of either beef or pork.) Brown the meat. Add a combination of flour and water for a thickened mixture to meat and continue to brown. Add chiles and garlic, salt and pepper, adding water as needed. Simmer for 30 to 40 minutes. (Serves 4 to 6)

Yeager's Beer Chili

Dick Yeager -- Cupertino, California

8 to 10 strips lean BACON (cubed)
4 lbs. STEW MEAT
3 med. ONIONS
3 stalks CELERY
2 lg. GREEN BELL PEPPERS
3 lg. cloves GARLIC
Leftover cooked MEATS*
1 cup Premium BEER
6 whole CLOVES
6-oz. CHILI POWDER

1 can (6-oz.) TOMATO PASTE
2 cans (28-oz.) and 1 can (16-oz.)
   TOMATOES
1 GREEN CHILI (hottest) diced
1 Tbsp. SALT
1 Tbsp. PAPRIKA
2 lg. BAY LEAVES

(*For leftover meats, use cooked beef, pork, venison, etc. in your freezer. Bones are OK. Remove excess fat.)

In large Dutch oven, cook cubed bacon over medium heat. Stir often, until bacon separates and starts to curl. Add stew meat (VERY coarsely ground premium meat), onions (VERY coarsely chopped), celery and peppers (coarsely chopped) and garlic (finely chopped). Cook until meat browns. Stir often and drain fat. Add leftover meats, beer, cloves, chili powder and tomato paste. Stir thoroughly. Add tomatoes with liquid, hot green chili, salt and paprika. Stir thoroughly, breaking up tomatoes with spoon. Add bay leaves. Stir again. Simmer, covered, four hours. Uncover and simmer another one to two hours. Stir occasionally. Remove any bones from leftover meat. (Serves 4)

Eldon Rudd's Chile con Carne

Congressman Eldon Rudd -- 4th District, Arizona

1½ lbs. BEEF (coarse ground)
1 lg. ONION (chopped)
1 GREEN PEPPER (chopped)
1 to 2 Tbsp. CHILI POWDER
1 can (28-oz.) TOMATOES
1 can (8-oz.) TOMATO SAUCE
1 can (8-oz.) WATER
GARLIC POWDER to taste
SALT and PEPPER
1 Tbsp. MILLERS BRAN
(optional)

Brown beef in Dutch oven. Add other ingredients, except bran. Simmer one hour, adding water if mixture is too thick. Add bran last ten minutes of cooking for flavor. (Serves 4 to 6)

Working Women's Chili

Mrs. Wayne Nelson -- Tucson, Arizona

2 Tbsp. BACON DRIPPINGS
2 cups ONIONS (chopped)
2 med. GREEN PEPPERS
¼ lb. MUSHROOMS (sliced thin)
1 lb. GROUND ROUND
½ lb. BULK SAUSAGE
4 Tbsp. CHILI POWDER
½ tsp. SALT
1/8 tsp. BLACK PEPPER
1 tsp. CUMIN
1 tsp. OREGANO
1 can (28-oz.) TOMATOES
½ cup COLD WATER

Heat bacon drippings in large frypan (or electric frypan). Add onions. Seed and chop green peppers and add. Stir-fry until tender. Add mushrooms, stirring until tender.

Add beef and sausage and stir-fry, breaking the meat with a spoon. Cook until meat is no longer pink. Stir in chili powder, salt, pepper, cumin, and oregano. Chop tomatoes into small pieces and add to mixture. Add water, stir, cover, and simmer 25 minutes. Uncover, stir, and simmer 15 minutes more (until slightly thickened). (Serves 6)

Cimarron "Simmer On"

Bert W. Huls -- Los Angeles, California

2 lbs. ground BEEF
2 Tbsp. SHORTENING
1½ cups ONIONS (chopped)
1 can (10¼-oz.) BEEF GRAVY
1 can (16-oz.) stewed TOMATOES
2 Tbsp. CHILI POWDER
1 tsp. KITCHEN BOUQUET
2 tsp. Lawry's SEASONED SALT
1 tsp. Worcestershire Sauce
6 oz. BEEFAMATO
2 Tbsp. Apple Cider VINEGAR
¼ tsp. GARLIC POWDER
¼ tsp. BLACK PEPPER
¼ tsp. CUMIN

Saute beef and onions in shortening until beef is gray and onions translucent. Drain off excess fat. While beef and onions are sauteing, place remaining ingredients in blender and blend thoroughly. Pour into three-quart saucepan. Add beef-onion mixture. Cover pan and simmer two hours. If thicker chili is desired, mix one tablespoon flour with enough cold water to make a thin paste and stir into chili. (To substitute: use table salt for Lawry's, V-8 or water for Beefamato, burgundy for vinegar.) (Makes two quarts)

Skipper's Chili

Bernice Hinds -- Concord, California

3 lbs. BEEF CHUCK (bite size)
3 med. ONIONS (chopped)
1 BELL PEPPER (chopped)
2 cloves GARLIC (crushed)
½ tsp. OREGANO
¼ tsp. CUMIN SEED
2 cans (6-oz.) TOMATO PASTE
1 quart WATER
2 Tbsp. CHILI POWDER
Salt and Pepper

Brown beef cubes and add remaining ingredients. Simmer 1 1/2 hours. Taste, re-season if necessary, let stand several hours and reheat. (Serves 6)

Cincinnati Chili

Barbara Rutti -- Scottsdale, Arizona

2 lbs. ground BEEF
4 med. ONIONS (chopped)
1 clove GARLIC (minced)
2 tsp. VINEGAR
1 can (12-oz.) TOMATO PASTE
2 to 3 Tbsp. CHILI POWDER
3 tsp. CINNAMON
1 tsp. TABASCO
2 dashes Worcestershire Sauce
1 quart WATER
SALT and PEPPER

Spice Bag
4 DRY PEPPERS
35 ALLSPICE
5 BAY LEAVES

Plus: hot cooked spaghetti, shredded sharp cheese, chopped onions, oyster crackers.

Saute beef, onions and garlic. Add all other ingredients. Simmer, partially covered, one hour. Remove spice bag. To serve, assemble by layers: hot spaghetti, topped by chili, cheese, onions, and oyster crackers. (Serves 6 to 8)

Chili Hot & Spicy

Louella Benton -- Santa Maria, California

1 lb. ground BEEF
2 Tbsp. CHILI POWDER
1¼ tsp. SALT
1½ cloves GARLIC (minced)
OR
¼ tsp. GARLIC POWDER

1 med. ONION (chopped)
¼ tsp. BLACK PEPPER
¼ tsp. CAYENNE
1 tsp. CUMIN
1 tsp. OREGANO
4 Tbsp. FLOUR
2 cups TOMATO JUICE

Brown ground beef. Add seasonings and flour. Mix well and stir in tomato juice. Bring chili to a boil, stirring occasionally. Reduce heat and simmer 15 to 20 minutes. (Serves 4 to 6)

A monthly newspaper devoted exclusively to news of chili cookoffs and chili happenings is the *Goat Gap Gazette,* 5110 Bayard Lane, #2, Houston, Texas 77006. One-year subscription is $11; Canadian subscriptions $16 U.S.; and U.S. overseas $22.

Palmer Hoyt's Chili

Palmer Hoyt -- Denver, Colorado

2 lbs. ground BEEF
¼ lb. SWEET SUET
1 quart WATER
4 Tbsp. CHILI POWDER
½ tsp. RED PEPPER (ground)
½ tsp. CUMIN (ground)
½ tsp. MARJORAM (powdered)
2 Tbsp. PAPRIKA
About 2 tsp. SALT
8 cloves GARLIC (chopped fine)
4 to 6 Tbsp. CRACKER MEAL

COLORADO

Have meat coarsely chopped or ground. Use good quality, firm (Colorado) beef, without fat or gristle. Fry out suet, remove cracklins, then saute meat over high heat until gray, stirring constantly. Add one quart water and simmer two hours. Add remaining ingredients EXCEPT garlic and cracker meal. Simmer 15 minutes more. Add garlic and simmer 30 minutes more. Remove from heat and stir in cracker meal. (If chili is too thick, add hot water for desired consistency. If thickening does not absorb all red grease, skim off that which remains on top.) (Serves 4 to 6)

Chuckwagon Chili

Bette L. Gregorio -- San Pedro, California

½ lb. BACON (diced)
2 lbs. lean BEEF (¾" cubes)
1 cup ONION (chopped)
1 clove GARLIC (minced)
2 cans (15-oz.) TOMATO SAUCE
1 Tbsp. Cider VINEGAR
1 Tbsp. BROWN SUGAR
3 Tbsp. CHILI POWDER
1 cup Stuffed OLIVES

Fry bacon in large pot until crisp and brown. Drain bacon on paper towel; pour off all but about three tablespoons of bacon drippings; set aside. Brown meat (about 1/3 at a time) in bacon drippings; set aside. Fry onion and garlic in the same pan. Add browned beef cubes, tomato sauce, vinegar, sugar and chili powder. Cover and simmer 2 1/2 hours (or until meat is tender), stirring occasionally. Add fried bacon and olives to pot 15 minutes before end of cooking. (Serves 6 to 8)

California Chili

Courtesy McIlhenny Co., mfrs. TABASCO Brand Pepper Sauce

2 lbs. ground BEEF
2 cups ONIONS (chopped)
1 cup GREEN PEPPER (diced)
2 cloves GARLIC (minced)
¼ cup CHILI POWDER
1 tsp. EACH of SALT, PAPKIKA,
    OREGANO & ground CUMIN
1 to 2 tsp. TABASCO Pepper Sauce
1 tsp. INSTANT COFFEE powder
1 can (8-oz.) TOMATO SAUCE
1 can (16-0z.) TOMATOES
1 cup WATER

In large, heavy saucepan, break up ground beef. Add onions, green pepper and garlic; cook, stirring frequently, until beef is browned and vegetables are tender. Add chili powder, salt, paprika, oregano, ground cumin, Tabasco, coffee, tomatoes, tomato sauce and water. Stir to mix well. Bring to a boil, reduce heat. Simmer, uncovered, 45 minutes or until thickened. (Serves 6 to 8)

Ray Neal's Venison Chili

Ray Neal -- Shreveport, Louisiana

½ cup OLIVE OIL
4 lbs. VENISON (¾" cubes)
½ cup BEEF SUET
2 cups ONION (minced)
2 BELL PEPPERS (chopped)
2 cloves GARLIC (chopped)
4 Tbsp. CHILI POWDER
2 Tbsp. PAPRIKA
1 can (16-oz.) whole TOMATOES
    (mashed)
2 cans TOMATO PASTE
1 cup WATER
SALT and PEPPER

Heat oil until smoky hot. Add venison and suet and stir til brown. Add onions, green peppers and garlic and continue cooking about five minutes. Add remaining ingredients and simmer until tender (about 1 1/2 hours. Add water as needed. Serves 6)

Herb's Chili

Betty Nelson -- Tucson, Arizona

2 Tbsp. BUTTER
4 Tbsp. OLIVE OIL
1 cup ONIONS (chopped)
2 lg. GARLIC CLOVES (minced)
4 Tbsp. FLOUR
2 lbs. BEEF CHUCK (1" cubes)
1 lb. PORK LOIN (1" cubes)
2 tsp. SALT
4 Tbsp. CHILI POWDER
1 tsp. OREGANO
1 tsp. ground CUMIN
2½ cups (13-oz. can) TOMATO PUREE
1 cup WHITE WINE
2 Tbsp. SESAME SEEDS
1 Tbsp. PARSLEY (chopped)
18 ripe OLIVES (pitted)
½ oz. Unsweetened CHOCOLATE

Heat butter and olive oil in frying pan. Add onions and saute til golden. Then add garlic cloves, and cook three minutes more. Dredge flour over onions and garlic. Push mixture to one side of frying pan. Quickly sear the cubed meat on the other side of frying pan. Add salt, chili powder, oregano, cumin, tomato puree and white wine. Mix seasoned meat and onions together, cover, and simmer for one hour. Uncover, test meat; if not tender, cook another 25 minutes. Add sesame seeds, parsley, and unsweetened chocolate, and stir mixture. Simmer for 25 minutes. Add olives and simmer 10 minutes more. (Serves 8)

Alma's Chili for a Crowd

Alma Coffelt -- Sacramento, California

3 lbs. SUET
2 Tbsp. SALT
4 tsp. ground RED PEPPER
4 Tbsp. GARLIC POWDER
1 lg. ONION (diced)
10 lbs. GROUND BEEF
2 heaping tsp. CHILI POWDER
3 Tbsp. COMINO SEEDS

Melt suet. Add salt, pepper, garlic powder, and onion, and cook five minutes. Add ground meat and cook until done, stirring occasionally. Add chili powder and comino. Simmer, the longer the better. (Makes 40 to 50 servings.)

Grandma's Chili
Valeria Paszli -- Litchfield Park, Arizona

OIL (for frying)
2 lg. ONIONS (chopped)
2 lbs. ground BEEF
1 lb. ground PORK
1 CHICKEN BREAST (ground)
2 Green CHILI PEPPERS (chopped)
½ cup CELERY (chopped)
2 GARLIC CLOVES (mashed)
2 pkgs. Lawry's CHILI MIX
1 Tbsp. SALT
1 can (28-oz.) stewed TOMATOES

Saute onions in a little oil. Add beef, pork, chicken, and cook for about one-half hour. Stir often. Add peppers, celery and mashed garlic and continue stirring. Add chili mix, tomatoes and salt and cook slowly for two or three hours. (Water may be added if mixture seems too thick.) (Makes about a gallon of medium hot chili.)

Judy's--A Chili To Remember
Judy L. Dunbar -- Phoenix, Arizona

3½ lbs. lean PORK
4 lbs. BEEF
2 tsp. OREGANO
5 cups ONIONS (chopped)
2½ cups CELERY (chopped fine)
2 BELL PEPPERS (chopped)
2 cans (28-oz.) Hunts TOMATO SAUCE
4 cans (14-oz.) Hunts Stewed TOMATOES
6 tsp. dehyd. GARLIC
1 JALAPENO PEPPER (chopped)
2 tsp. crushed RED PEPPER
4 tsp. CUMIN
6 tsp. mild CHILI POWDER
3 tsp. VEGETABLE FLAKES
SALT (to taste)

Have meat coarse ground for chili. Brown meat until gray. Drain (if necessary). Add oregano, onions, celery and peppers and finish browning until onions are tender. Add remaining ingredients. Mix well, cover, and simmer three hours, stirring occasionally. (This chili is not hot.) (Serves 10 to 12)

Hightower's Awful Good Texas Chili

Jim Hightower -- Austin, Texas

3 strips thick BACON
3 lbs. lean BEEF (coarse ground)
1 medium ONION (chopped fine)
3 medium cloves GARLIC (minced)
1 can (6-oz.) TOMATO PASTE
3 Tbsp. ground CUMIN
1 Tbsp. ground OREGANO
1 Tbsp. SALT
1 Tbsp. ground black PEPPER
1 bottle (12-oz.) BEER*
6 to 9 dried Red CHILI PODS
3 cups WATER

(*Dark Mexican beer is best)

In a large, cast-iron kettle, fry bacon crisp. Remove and discard bacon, saving the grease. Add meat, onion and garlic and saute in bacon grease until meat is grey. Stir in tomato paste, then add spices and mix well through the meat. Pour in beer. Stir thoroughly and remove from heat.

Remove stems and seeds from dried chili pods. Boil in a covered saucepan with water for 15 minutes. Put peppers and water into blender and blend into thick sauce; pour sauce into kettle with meat; stir in and simmer for two hours. (Check after 1 1/2 hours. If chili needs thickening, add a tablespoon of Masa Harina. If chili is too thick, add water sparingly. For hotter chili, add cayenne pepper or Tabasco sauce--sparingly.) (Serves 8)

Ruth's Deer Chili

Ruth Hartwell -- Dixon, California

3 lbs. SUET
12 lbs. DEER MEAT (chili grind)
6 long RED PEPPERS
6 tsp. CAYENNE Pepper
½ cup GROUND GARLIC
2 jars (2-oz.) Grandma's Spanish
Chili Seasonings
SALT to taste

Render suet first in a large, heavy pan. Then add meat and cook slowly for two hours, stirring often. Add red peppers and cook 30 minutes. Add garlic, and cook 30 minutes longer. Add salt, cayenne, and chili seasonings. Cook 10 minutes longer. Pour into 12"x15"x2" pan. Refrigerate overnight. Cut into blocks and freeze. (Each block should serve two. Add water to blocks when reheating.) (Serves 8 to 10)

Texts Chili

United States Senator John Tower -- Texas

3 lbs. CHILI MEAT
1 can (15-oz.) TOMATO SAUCE
1 can (15-oz.) WATER
1 tsp. TABASCO
3 heaping Tbsp. CHILI POWDER (Pure)
1 heaping Tbsp. OREGANO
1 heaping tsp. CUMINO POWDER
2 ONIONS (chopped)
GARLIC to taste
1 tsp. SALT
1 tsp. CAYENNE POWDER
1 level tsp. PAPRIKA
1 doz. Red Jap PEPPERS
4 or 5 Dried Ancho CHILI PODS
2 heaping tsp. FLOUR

Sear meat until gray. Add tomato sauce and one cup of water. Add other ingredients. Simmer for 1 1/4 hours. Add thickening (flour mixed with water). Simmer an additional 30 minutes. (Serves 6 to 8)

Mom Unser's Ortega Green Chile

Courtesy Heublein, Inc., Grocery Products Group

1 lb. lean PORK SHOULDER (¼" cubes)
2 Tbsp. FLOUR
2 Tbsp. LARD (or shortening)
½ cup ONION (chopped)
1 clove GARLIC (minced)
1 can (16-oz.) whole TOMATOES
   (chopped coarse)
4 cans (4-oz.) OR 2 cans (7-oz.)
   Ortega Diced GREEN CHILES
½ tsp. OREGANO
2½ tsp. SALT
2 cups WATER

Dredge meat in flour. Melt lard in large, deep skillet. Brown meat thoroughly. Add onion and garlic, and cook until onion is soft. Add remaining ingredients. Simmer, covered, from 1 to 2 hours, stirring occasionally. Remove cover. Simmer, uncovered, 5 to 10 minutes. (Serves 4 to 6)

Mountain Venison Chili

Virginia A. McCann -- Boulder, Colorado

2 lbs. cooked VENISON (ground)
1 quart VENISON BROTH or Water
2 med. ONIONS (chopped fine)
1 can (15-oz.) TOMATO SAUCE
1 tsp. ALLSPICE
1 tsp. CORIANDER (ground)
1 to 2 BAY LEAVES
½ tsp. crushed RED PEPPER
1 tsp. CUMIN (ground)
4 cloves GARLIC (minced)
2 Tbsp. RED VINEGAR (apple)
4 Tbsp. CHILI POWDER
2 tsp. SALT
½ oz. Unsweetened Baking CHOCOLATE
1 tsp. CINNAMON
1 cup SOUR CREAM
1 cup CHUTNEY

In a large pot, add ground venison to broth (or water). Stir until venison separates. Boil slowly for 30 minutes. Add all other ingredients EXCEPT sour cream and chutney. Stir to blend. Bring mixture to a boil. Reduce heat and simmer uncovered for three hours. Pot may be covered last hour, after desired consistency is reached. Remove bay leaves. Serve with side dishes of sour cream and chutney. (Serves 6-8)

Margarete's Hot Chili

Margarete Lockley -- Farmington, New Mexico

1 med. ONION (grated)
OIL for sauteing
1 lb. CHILI MEAT
1 clove GARLIC (mashed)
Dash of CAYENNE
3 Tbsp. CHILI POWDER
3 Tbsp. FLOUR (or Cornstarch)
1 can (#303) TOMATOES
WATER as needed

Heat oil, saute grated onion. Add meat and stir until redness leaves. Drain grease thoroughly. Add mashed garlic, cayenne, chili powder (use blended powder), and stir well. Add flour (or cornstarch) slowly and stir. Mash tomatoes into pieces, add to meat mixture and stir. Add water, cover completely, and simmer one hour. Stir occasionally for an hour. (Serves 6)

Buzzard's Breath Chili

Tom Griffin -- Houston, Texas
World Champion, Arriba Terlingua, Texas

8 lbs. BEEF (U.S. choice boneless chuck)
3 cans (8-oz.) TOMATO SAUCE
2 large ONIONS (chopped)
5 cloves GARLIC (crushed and chopped)
2 JALAPEÑO peppers
CHILI POWDER (about twice label amount)
2 tsp. CUMIN (ground)
¼ to ½ tsp. OREGANO
SALT to taste
1 to 2 tsp. PAPRIKA
CAYENNE pepper (to taste)
MASA HARINA (as needed)
1 qt. BEEF STOCK

Take meat and chop into 3/8" cubes, removing all gristle and visible fat. Brown in an iron skillet (about 2 lbs. at a time) until gray in color. Place in a large, cast-iron chili pot, adding tomato sauce and equal amounts of water. Add chopped onion, garlic, jalapeño peppers (wrapped in cheese cloth), and chili powder.

Simmer for 20 minutes, then add cumin, oregano, salt and cayenne pepper to taste. As moisture is required, add homemade beef stock until amount used, then add water if needed.

Simmer covered until meat is tender (about two hours), stirring occasionally. Then add Masa Harina to achieve desired thickness if needed. Add paprika for color. Cook 10 additional minutes, correct seasoning to taste, discard jalapeños and serve.

A small additional amount of cumin enhances aroma when added in last ten minutes. (Serves 12)

Hot Chili

Omie Marchbanks -- Levelland, Texas

2 Tbsp. COOKING OIL
4 lbs. CHILI MEAT
3 tsp. SALT
4 Tbsp. CHILI POWDER
1½ tsp. RED PEPPER
2 Tbsp. PAPRIKA

6 cloves GARLIC
1 tsp. CUMIN
¼ cup CRACKER MEAL or
   2 Tbsp. FLOUR
3 or 4 cups TOMATO JUICE or
   WATER

Cook meat in oil until it changes color. Drain off excess fats. Add all other ingredients and simmer for 1 1/2 to 2 hours. For milder chili, omit red pepper. (Serves 6 to 8)

Mouth of Hell Chili

Jo Ann Horton, editor *Goat Gap Gazette*

1 large ONION (chopped)
2 Tbsp. OIL
2 lbs. lean CHILI MEAT (chili grind)
1 can (16-oz.) TOMATOES
2 cans (8-oz.) TOMATO SAUCE
1 tsp. SUGAR
2 tsp. ground CUMIN
2 tsp. PAPRIKA
2 large cloves GARLIC (crushed)
1 can BEER
2 fresh JALAPENO PEPPERS (finely minced)
5 Tbsp. CHILI POWDER
Salt & Cayenne Pepper to taste

Saute onion in oil. Add chili meat and stir until gray. Add remaining ingredients and cook until thick (about 1½ hours). The "hotness" of the chili will depend on how much cayenne pepper is used. (Serves 4 to 6). To make an enchilada casserole, layer warm chili with grated cheese and onions and corn tortillas in a baking dish. Bake at 350 F for 15-20 minutes. Cut into squares and serve.

Logan and Jo's Hideaway Chili

Logan Howe & Jo Greenwell -- Avondale, Arizona

6 lbs. lean MEAT (½" cubes)
1 lg. pkg. Farmer John Bulk
  PORK SAUSAGE
OLIVE OIL
3 ONIONS (diced)
2 whole cloves GARLIC
BUTTER
2 lbs. peeled TOMATOES
2 cans (8-oz.) TOMATO SAUCE
2 cans (4-oz.) diced GREEN
  CHILES

2 Tbsp. CHILI POWDER
1 tsp. PAPRIKA
2½ tsp. SALT
2 tsp. ACCENT
3 tsp. PEPPER
2 tsp. OREGANO
2 tsp. TABASCO
1 can BEER
1 cup CELERY (diced)
1 tsp. ANISE
3 JALAPENOS

Brown meat and pork in small amount of olive oil. Saute onion and garlic in butter. Combine all ingredients in a two-gallon pot, EXCEPT jalapenos. Cook, uncovered, for about three hours. Slice two jalapenos on the sides, but DO NOT cut in half. Dice one jalapeno. Add jalapenos to chili mixture, and remove with tongs or slotted spoon when chili is spicy enough. (Makes 1 gallon)

Bandito Chili

John W. Eckert -- Phoenix, Arizona

4 strips BACON
3 cloves GARLIC
5 lbs. LEAN BEEF (coarse ground)
2 lbs. ONIONS (chopped)
6 whole GREEN CHILES
5 tsp. CHILI POWDER
3 lbs. TOMATOES
8 dashes PEPPER SAUCE
1 tsp. OREGANO
1 tsp. CUMIN
2 cups RED WINE
2 tsp. SWEET BASIL

Cut bacon into squares, place in bottom of Dutch oven or heavy pot, and heat. (This renders the bacon.) Add garlic cloves, lean beef, onions and stir. Chop whole chiles into small pieces and add. After meat mixture has browned, add spices and tomatoes. Then add wine, bring to a boil, and simmer for two hours. (Makes one gallon)

Es Not Too Bad Chili

Bill Gere -- Avondale, Arizona

7 lbs. GROUND BEEF (coarse)
2 Tbsp. PAPRIKA
6 med. ONIONS (chopped)
1 WHOLE GARLIC (chopped)
BUTTER
2 Tbsp. CUMIN
2 oz. CHILI POWDER
3 JALAPENO PEPPERS (chopped)
¼ tsp. Mexican-Style OREGANO
3 cans (16-oz.) whole TOMATOES
2 cans (#10) TOMATO SAUCE
Garlic Salt, Salt & Pepper

Brown meat with paprika in a cast iron skillet. Saute onions and garlic in butter in a separate pan. Combine onions and garlic with meat in a 13-quart pot. Add remaining ingredients and simmer four hours, stirring regularly. (Serves 8)

4-K Chili

Ed "Chill Lee" Paetzel -- The Chill Lee Corp., Alief, Texas

     5 lbs. Lean MEAT
     1 lg. ONION (chopped fine)
     3 cloves GARLIC (chopped fine)
     1 lg. Canned JALAPENO (chopped with seeds)
     1 pkg. CHILL LEE'S CHILI MIX
     2 Tbsp. CUMIN
     2 Tbsp. New Mexico CHILI POWDER
     1 tsp. PAPRIKA
     1 tsp. Ground BLACK PEPPER
     1 tsp. ACCENT (MSG)
     1 tsp. SALT
     1 can (15-oz.) Hunts TOMATO SAUCE
     1 can of BEER
     16-oz. WATER

Use enough oil to lightly cover bottom of pan. Brown meat. Brown onion, garlic and jalapeno together. (If using fresh jalapeno, remove the seeds.)

Before adding liquid, mix onion, garlic, jalapeno, Chili Mix, and spices in with meat and stir in well. Add tomato sauce, beer and water. Stir well.

(Chili ground meat should cook for at least two hours. Hand-cut meat should be cooked for three to four hours. Hamburger meat, after browning, should be ready in about an hour. The seasoning starts to work in about 45 minutes.) (Serves 6 to 8)

Mo's Chili

Elmo J. Hudgins -- San Jose, California

  2 lbs. CHUCK (coarse grind)
  2 cups TOMATO JUICE
  2 oz. CHILI POWDER
  1 med. ONION (chopped)
  ½ tsp. BLACK PEPPER

  ½ tsp. CUMIN (ground)
  2 sm. cloves GARLIC
  ¼ cup MASA FLOUR
  ½ tsp. RED PEPPER

Put meat into heavy skillet (or cast iron pot). Cook all the moisture out of meat (until slightly browned). Add tomato juice and water. Simmer until meat begins to show signs of tenderness. Add chili powder, onion, salt, black pepper, cumin and garlic cloves. Continue to cook until meat is thoroughly tender. Put masa flour into mixing cup, add water to thin, gravy consistency. Add to chili and stir until well mixed. (For added "hot" flavor, add 1/2 teaspoon red pepper.)(Serves 8)

Rudy Valdez Chili

Rudy Valdez—Albuquerque, New Mexico
1976 World Champion at International Chili Society Cookoff

1 lb. PORK SHOULDER (chopped into ⅜" pieces)
1 lb. BEEF FLANK STEAK (chopped very fine, but not ground)
1 tsp. CUMIN
1 medium WHITE ONION
1 ripe TOMATO (chopped)
6 sticks CELERY (6" long, chopped)
1 can (8 oz.) Ortega GREEN CHILE SALSA
1 can (8 oz.) Ortega GREEN CHILE PEPPERS (diced)
1 clove GARLIC (minced)
1 tsp. OREGANO
1 tsp. TABASCO SAUCE
1 Tbsp. hot New Mexico CHILI POWDER
1 Tbsp. medium New Mexico CHILI POWDER
1 Tbsp. mild New Mexico CHILI POWDER
(Use heaping tablespoonsful)
SALT to taste

Cook pork and beef in separate pans for 20 minutes. Add ½ teaspoon of cumin to each skillet. In a 6-quart saucepan combine remaining ingredients EXCEPT for chili powder and salt. With the three grades of chili powder, make a paste by adding a small amount of water. Add to vegetable mixture in the saucepan. Cook this mixture for twenty minutes. Drain the juice from the meat EXCEPT for four tablespoons, and add to the vegetable mixture. Cook for about 1½ hours until meat is tender. Just prior to serving, add salt according to taste.

Chilli* Recipe

Joe DeFrates—Springfield, Illinois
1973 & 1975 World Champion at International Chili Society Cookoff

1¼ oz. envelope Chilli Man CHILLI MIX
1 lb. GROUND BEEF
1 can (8 oz.) TOMATO SAUCE
1 dash TABASCO SAUCE

Follow directions on package. Do not add beans or water.

*According to Mr. DeFrates, chiliheads in Illinois spell chili with two "ll's."

A paean for the bean is long overdue. Beans are simple to cook, easy to store, low in cost, and nutritious as well. Since the protein of beans is incomplete, the most nourishment can be achieved by serving them with cheese, milk or meat. Thus, chili with beans makes sense from a health standpoint, as well as taste.

Recipes for Chili with Beans

Beans, too, are an excellent meal extender; a pound of dry beans will provide from eight to ten servings (allowing about one-fourth cup of dry beans per portion).

Several popular ways to prepare beans include: (1) straight boiling, (2) soaking and then boiling, (3) pressure cooking and (4) crockery cooking.

The simplest method is the straight boil. After beans have been washed and sorted (to discard debris and immature beans) they are put up to cook in boiling water. The ratio is one part beans to three parts water. Beans are then cooked until tender, about four to five hours.

Bean soaking can be accomplished in two ways. Beans can be boiled for two minutes, removed from the heat, and soaked for one hour before actual cooking (using the soaking water for cooking purposes). Or, beans can be soaked overnight to cut down on actual cooking time. However, it is suggested that beans be boiled for two minutes before the overnight soaking to keep them from souring.

As for salt, about one teaspoon per cup of beans is considered adequate. The quantity of salt can be reduced, of course, if salt pork or ham is used. Salt itself should be added only 30 minutes before beans are done. To add salt earlier invites the possibility of hard beans.

Beans should be cooked until they are tender and plump but still whole, rather than broken or mushy. If the skin of the bean is tough, the bean is not thoroughly cooked.

During the cooking period, some types of beans have a tendency to foam up high. To reduce this foaming, add a tablespoon of fat to the water for each cup of beans used (an especially useful tip for pressure cookers).

To heighten bean color, a pinch of baking soda can be employed, though not recommended for nutritive value. A more distinctive touch is a tablespoon of peanut butter added to a simmering pot of beans.

Since the Spanish word for beans is "frijoles," the chili recipes which include beans are often identified as "chile con carne con frijoles" or "chile con frijoles."

Texas Chili with Beans

Courtesy McIlhenny Co.,mfrs. TABASCO Brand Pepper Sauce

1 lb. dried PINTO BEANS
¼ cup SALAD OIL
3 lbs. STEW MEAT (1" cubes)
3 lg. ONIONS (chopped)
3 cloves GARLIC (minced)
1/3 cup CHILI POWDER
2 tsp. SALT
3 tsp. TABASCO Pepper Sauce
1 tsp. ground CUMIN
1 tsp. PAPRIKA
1 can (8-oz.) TOMATO SAUCE
1 can (6-oz.) TOMATO PASTE
1 quart WATER

Soak beans overnight in water to cover. Drain, place in saucepan and cover generously with cold water. Bring to a boil, cover, reduce heat and simmer two hours. Heat oil in large saucepan and add beef, onions and garlic. Cook until meat is browned. Add remaining ingredients; stir to mix well. Bring to a boil and reduce heat. Simmer, uncovered, two hours (or until meat is tender.) Stir occasionally. Stir in drained beans before serving chili. (Serves 8 to 10)

Alta Lamb's Chili

Alta Lamb -- Phoenix, Arizona

2 cups PINTO BEANS
1 quart WATER
1 lb. GROUND CHUCK
2 Tbsp. SHORTENING
½ cup ONIONS (chopped)
½ cup KETCHUP
½ cup WATER
1 Tbsp. SALT
2 Tbsp. SUGAR
2 Tbsp. CHILI POWDER

Soak pinto beans in water overnight. In the morning, wash beans twice. Cover with water. Bring to a full boil. Reduce heat and simmer 1 1/2 hours.

Heat shortening in a skillet. Add meat and onions, stirring continuously with a fork until meat turns gray. Add remaining ingredients and simmer 30 minutes. Combine meat mixture with beans and simmer 30 minutes more. (Serves 4 to 6)

Bite-the-Bullet Locomotive Chili

Erin Thompson -- Santa Cruz, California

1/3 lb. PINTO BEANS
1/3 lb. KIDNEY BEANS
1/3 lb. Red or Pink BEANS
OLIVE OIL
1 lb. CHUCK (cubed)
2 ONIONS
4 cloves GARLIC
½ GREEN PEPPER
1/3 lb. MUSHROOMS
1 lg. stalk CELERY
3 cans (14½-oz.) stewed Italian
    TOMATOES
1 BAY LEAF
¼ cup fresh BASIL
¼ cup fresh PARSLEY
4 level Tbsp. CHILI POWDER
3 level Tbsp. CUMIN
1 Tbsp. OREGANO
1 tsp. CAYENNE
1 Tbsp. MARJORAM
1 Tbsp. SUGAR
2 cans (8-oz.) TOMATO PASTE
SALT to taste

Combine beans and soak overnight in water to cover. Rinse beans next morning and set aside. Crush garlic. Slice mushrooms and celery. Chop onions, green pepper, basil and parsley separately.

In a large Dutch oven, heat oil and brown meat, onions, garlic, green pepper, mushrooms and celery until meat is cooked. Add rinsed beans to meat. Crush Italian tomatoes (use hands or electric beater) to keep seeds intact. Add tomatoes, spices, and water (if needed) to barely cover. Simmer for at least an hour (until meat is tender). Turn off flame and stir in tomato paste. Taste and correct seasonings.

(Seeds of the Italian tomatoes should not be broken, for they may turn chili bitter. Adding tomato paste AFTER flame is turned off prevents chili from becoming bitter.) (Serves 10 to 20)

Sallie Hayden's Chili

Courtesy Hayden Flour Mills -- Tempe, Arizona

2 cups (1 pkg.) Rose Brand PINTO or Red KIDNEY BEANS
WATER for soaking
1 quart FRESH WATER
1 Tbsp. SALT

Wash and pick over beans. In a deep bowl, cover beans generously with water and soak overnight. Drain. Cover and simmer beans in a heavy 4-quart kettle with one quart fresh water and one tablespoon salt for 1 1/2-hours.

3 or 4 slices BACON
1 lb. GROUND BEEF
2 Tbsp. BACON DRIPPINGS
2 cloves GARLIC (crushed)
1½ cans TOMATO PUREE
1 can CONSOMME (undiluted)

4 tsp. CHILI POWDER
½ tsp. OREGANO
¼ tsp. SAGE
¼ tsp. CUMIN SEED
2 Tbsp. BUTTER
2 cups ONION (chopped)
½ cup GREEN PEPPER (diced)

Saute bacon and drain bacon strips on paper towel. Brown ground beef in bacon drippings. Add browned beef with garlic, tomato puree, consomme, chili powder, oregano, sage and cumin seed to simmering beans. Re-cover and continue simmering. Saute chopped onion and green pepper in butter. When tender, add to beans and continue simmering (covered) for 2 1/2 to 3 hours (until beans are tender). Season to taste and garnish with crumbled bacon. (Serves 6 to 8)

Hearty, Old-Fashioned Chili

Tracy Young -- Richardson, Texas

2 lg. ONIONS (sliced)
2 GREEN PEPPERS (chopped)
2 lbs. GROUND BEEF
1 can (16-oz.) KIDNEY BEANS
2 cans (1 lb.) TOMATOES
2 cans (8-oz.) seasoned TOMATO
SAUCE
2 Tbsp. CHILI POWDER
2 tsp. SALT
Dash PAPRIKA and CAYENNE

Brown onion, green pepper and meat. Drain 1/2 liquid from kidney beans. Add beans and bean liquid and remaining ingredients. Pour into a saucepan, stir, cover, and simmer 1 1/2 hours stirring occasionally. (Serves 8 to 10)

Schmitt's Special Chili

United States Senator Harrison Schmitt -- New Mexico

1 cup cooked BEANS (and juice)
1 pint fresh CHILI PASTE
(no additives)
1 lb. GROUND BEEF
ROSEMARY, SAGE
PEPPER (fresh, coarse ground)
1 lg. fresh TOMATO
1 lg. fresh ONION
1 lg. fresh BELL PEPPER
Chopped GREEN CHILI

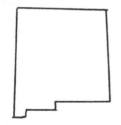

Combine chili paste and cooked beans in large pot and simmer. Panfry chunky ground beef (or pork) and season to taste
with spices while cooking. Add to simmering beans and stir.
Add vegetables (chopped coarsely) and chopped green chili.
Simmer about one hour. Add salt to taste. (Serves 4 to 6)

Bowl of Fire

Harold J. Kelly -- Tucson, Arizona

2 lbs. RED BEANS
3 lbs. GROUND BEEF (coarse)
¼ cup OLIVE OIL
1½ quarts WATER
8 Dry Red CHILI PODS *
3 tsp. SALT
10 cloves GARLIC (chopped fine)
1 tsp. CUMIN (ground)
1 tsp. OREGANO (or Marjoram)
1 tsp. RED PEPPER
1 Tbsp. SUGAR
3 Tbsp. PAPRIKA
3 Tbsp. FLOUR
6 Tbsp. CORN MEAL

Use red beans (not kidney beans) and soak overnight. Boil
next morning until tender and drain thoroughly. (This is a
must!) Add cooked beans to cooked chili.

Braise meat in olive oil until it turns gray (not brown).
Add water and simmer 1 1/2 hours. Add all ingredients
EXCEPT flour and corn meal. Cook 30 minutes more. Then
thicken with flour and corn meal mixed with one cup of water.
Stir into bubbling chili mixture and continue stirring to prevent
sticking. Cook five minutes more for consistency. (Serves 12)

* (Or substitute 6 tablespoons chili powder for pods.)

Tex-Mex Chili

Jewel Johnston -- San Jose, California

3 Tbsp. Vegetable OIL
3½ lbs. CHUCK ROAST (½" cubes)
3 cloves GARLIC (minced)
1 tsp. crushed, dry RED PEPPERS
6 Tbsp. CHILI POWDER
1½ tsp. CUMIN SEEDS
3 Tbsp. MASA
1 Tbsp. leaf OREGANO
2 tsp. SALT
½ tsp. BLACK PEPPER (coarse ground)
1 can (13-oz.) BEEF BROTH
1 can (8-oz.) TOMATO SAUCE
1 can (2-oz.) CHILI SALSA
3 cups cooked PINTO BEANS
Sharp CHEDDAR CHEESE

Use lean boneless chuck. Add oil to cubed beef, and mix to coat all pieces. Heat a Dutch oven, add oiled beef cubes and stir over medium heat until beef loses pink color, but do NOT brown! Stir in garlic and crushed red peppers. Remove from heat.

Combine chili powder, cumin seed, masa (or all-purpose flour), oregano, salt and black pepper and sprinkle over beef cubes until well coated. Slowly add broth and tomato sauce to meat, stirring until well blended.

Return to heat, bring almost to boil, then reduce heat to low. Cover and simmer 1 1/2 hours; stir occasionally. Add chili salsa and beans (drained), and simmer 30 minutes more. Serve in heated bowls; garnish with grated cheese. (Serves 6 to 8)

Aunt Gail's Chili

Gail Wilson -- Hollywood, California

1 lb. GROUND MEAT
¼ cup ONION (chopped)
2 Tbsp. Sweet PEPPER FLAKES
1 can (15-oz.) Hunt's Herb
  TOMATO SAUCE
1 cup Ragu SPAGHETTI Sauce

1 can (8-oz.) KIDNEY BEANS
3 cans (15-oz.) WATER
½ tsp. CHILI POWDER
1 Tbsp. SUGAR
1 can (4-oz.) Pet Old El Paso
  TACO SAUCE

Brown ground meat in large pan or casserole. Pour off excess grease. Add remaining ingredients. Bring to a slow boil. Turn heat down to simmer and simmer for about 1 1/2 hours, until thickened. (This is a "soupy" chili.) (Serves 8)

Chili-Ginger

Lou Ann Houser -- San Jose, California

1 Tbsp. Cider VINEGAR
2 Tbsp. WATER
4 (2" round Nabisco) GINGER COOKIES
2 Tbsp. SHORTENING
1 lb. GROUND BEEF
½ lb. lean GROUND PORK
1½ cups ONION (chopped)
1 cup CELERY (diced)
1 lg. clove GARLIC (minced)
1 med. GREEN PEPPER (chopped)
2 cups canned TOMATOES
1 to 2 Tbsp. CHILI POWDER
2 tsp. SALT
1 tsp. SUGAR
4 cups RED KIDNEY BEANS (cooked or canned)

Chop onion and green pepper separately. Dice the celery; mince the garlic. Soak ginger cookies in vinegar and water.

Melt shortening in large-sized, heavy pan. Add beef and pork, and cook, stirring until lightly browned. Add onion, celery, garlic, and green pepper. Continue to cook, stirring until onions are golden. Add tomatoes, chili powder, soaked ginger cookies, salt and sugar. When mixture begins to boil, put heat on low, cover, and simmer one hour. Drain beans and add to meat mixture. Continue to cook, uncovered, until chili is thoroughly heated. (Serves 8)

Babs Phillips Championship Chili

Babs (Mrs. Sam) Phillips -- Phoenix, Arizona

4 lbs. BEEF (cubed bite-size)
4 or 5 ONIONS (chopped)
2 cloves GARLIC (crushed)
2 Tbsp. CHILI POWDER
2 tsp. SALT
1 tsp. Ground OREGANO
1 tsp. CUMIN POWDER
2 cans (16-oz.) TOMATOES (chopped)
2 cups Hot WATER
1 can (30-oz.) CHILI BEANS (undrained)

In a large skillet, cook together meat, onion and garlic. Add chili powder, salt, oregano, cumin, tomatoes with juice and hot water. Mix well. Simmer about three hours. Add canned beans to chili about 45 minutes before serving. (Serves 8)

Chili Ricki

Rick Guido -- San Jose, California

½ lb. RED BEANS
½ lb. PINTO BEANS
6 cups WATER
2 Tbsp. Cooking OIL
1 ONION (chopped)
1 clove GARLIC (minced)
2 lbs. GROUND BEEF
1 BELL PEPPER (chopped)

3 tsp. SALT
¼ tsp. PEPPER
3 tsp. CHILI POWDER
1 tsp. PAPRIKA
¼ tsp. CUMIN
½ tsp. ORANGE PEEL (grated)
4 cups TOMATO JUICE

Wash beans, cover with water, and bring to a boil. Let stand one hour. Cover; simmer about two hours (until tender). Heat oil in a skillet, and cook onions and garlic until golden. Add meat and cook until meat separates and browns. Add meat mixture and remaining ingredients to beans. Simmer, uncovered about 1 1/2 hours, stirring occasionally. (Oils in the orange peel help to blend all the spices.) (Serves 12 to 16)

Rio Grande Chili

Courtesy McIlhenny Co., mfrs. TABASCO Brand Pepper Sauce

2 Tbsp. SALAD OIL
1 med. ONION (chopped)
1 clove GARLIC (crushed)
1 lb. Ground BEEF
2 tsp. SALT
1 tsp. PAPRIKA
2 tsp. CHILI POWDER
2 cans (1 lb. each) KIDNEY
  BEANS
½ cup BEAN LIQUID
1 can (16-oz.) stewed TOMATOES
1 can (6-oz.) TOMATO PASTE
½ tsp. SUGAR
¾ tsp. TABASCO Pepper Sauce
1 can (12-oz.) Whole Kernel CORN
  (drained)

Heat oil in large skillet; add onion and garlic and cook until yellow, but not brown. Add ground beef; sprinkle with salt, paprika and chili powder. Cook meat until brown, breaking up with a fork. Drain kidney beans and discard all but 1/2 cup liquid; reserve beans. Stir in bean liquid, tomatoes, tomato paste, sugar and Tabasco. Cover and simmer 30 minutes. Add beans and corn; simmer 15 minutes longer, stirring occasionally. Serve with rice and Tabasco Sauce on side. (Serves 6)

Arizona's Fine Chili

United States Senator Barry Goldwater -- Arizona

1 lb. PINTO BEANS*
1 lb. GROUND BEEF (coarse)
2 cups ONION (chopped)
1 can (6-oz.) TOMATO PUREE
3 Tbsp. CHILI POWDER
SALT to taste
1 Tbsp. CUMIN
WATER

*Beans can be soaked overnight, or--if added dry--chili must cook long enough for beans to tenderize.
Saute beef and drain off excess fat. Add onions, tomato puree and beans. Mix chili powder, salt and cumin and add to mixture. Bring to a boil, turn down heat and cook slowly until onions and beans are tender, adding water to desired consistency. (Serves 4)

Super Chili

Dorene L. Avritt -- Albuquerque, New Mexico

2 cups PINTO BEANS
2 lbs. GROUND BEEF
1 med. ONION (diced)
¼ cup FLOUR
¼ cup CHILE POWDER
2 quarts WATER
½ Tbsp. SALT
½ Tbsp. PEPPER
¾ tsp. GARLIC POWDER
1 tsp. OREGANO
½ tsp. WHOLE CUMIN
¼ tsp. CUMIN (ground)
4 dashes Lawry's SEASONED SALT
2 cans El Paso TOMATOES & GREEN CHILE
Fresh or canned GREEN CHILE to taste

Begin with uncooked beans. Cook beans by favorite method and salt.
In large pot, brown meat with onion. Spoon off all grease EXCEPT for 1/2 cup. Add flour and chile powder. Cook for one minute. Add two quarts water and cook to boiling point.
Add remaining ingredients and cooked beans (undrained). Cover, and simmer for one hour. (Makes 4 1/2 quarts)

Willie's Green Chile Chili

William D. Beatty -- Mesa, Arizona

1 lb. HAMBURGER
2 med. ONIONS (chopped)
2 cans (6-oz.) TOMATO PASTE
1 can (7¾-oz.) El Pato TOMATO
SAUCE

1 can (14-oz.) stewed TOMATOES
3 tsp. CHILI POWDER
1 can (4-oz.) chopped GREEN
CHILI
1 can (15-oz.) Red Kidney Beans

Pressure Cooker (4 qt.)

In a 4-quart pressure cooker, brown hamburger and chopped onion. Add juice from kidney beans, and remaining ingredients, EXCEPT chili and kidney beans. Cover and cook for 18 minutes after rocker begins. Fast cool, remove lid. Add chili and beans. Simmer (uncovered) 1/2 hour before serving. (Serves 4)

Covered Sauce Pan (4 qt.)

Brown hamburger and chopped onion. Add juice from kidney beans and remaining ingredients EXCEPT beans and green chile. Simmer, covered, for two hours.

Add green chile and beans. Simmer, uncovered, for one-half hour before serving. (Serves 4)

Sunday Night Chili

Alice Adamson -- Austin, Minnesota

1 cup ONION (chopped)
1 tsp. GARLIC (chopped)
1½ lbs. GROUND BEEF (coarse)
¾ lb. fresh MUSHROOMS (sliced)
1 tsp. SALT
2 Tbsp. CHILI POWDER
¼ cup WATER
½ cup CATSUP
2 cans BEEF Consomme
3 Tbsp. CORN STARCH
1 can (15-oz.) KIDNEY BEANS

Panfry onion, garlic and hamburger; drain (if necessary). Add mushrooms (fresh or canned), and salt, and cook for five minutes. Blend chili powder with two tablespoons water and add to meat mixture. Add catsup and consomme and heat to boil. Blend corn starch with remaining water and add to meat. Simmer 15 minutes. Add beans (undrained) and simmer 10 minutes more. (Serves 6)

Hog-Heaven Chili

Cathy Brown -- Richardson, Texas

1 lb. GROUND BEEF (chili-ground)
½ lb. "Hot" PORK SAUSAGE
   Roll
1 lg. ONION (chopped)
1 clove GARLIC (slivered)
1 can (10-oz.) TOMATO PASTE
1 can (13-oz.) TOMATOES &
   CHILES
1 can (16-oz.) stewed TOMATOES
1 can (16-oz.) PINTO BEANS
2 cans (16-oz.) KIDNEY BEANS

2 cans (16-oz.) WATER
1 Tbsp. CHILI POWDER
½ Tbsp. CUMIN
2 tsp. SALT
2 Tbsp. SUGAR
2 Tbsp. White VINEGAR
Dash of PEPPER
1 cup SHARP CHEDDAR (grated)
Sour Cream
Lime Wedges

In a heavy skillet, brown beef, sausage, chopped onion and garlic until meat is crumbly. Drain off grease. Place meat mixture in an 8-quart pot. Add remaining ingredients. Bring to a boil, stirring often, then simmer for three hours. (Vinegar and sugar should be added in equal amounts. Add more water as moisture cooks down.) Serve topped with sprinkled grated cheese and a dollop of sour cream. Squeeze lime wedges over chili to cut the "bite." (Serves 12)

Rita's Mexican Chili

Rita M. Mitchell -- Los Altos, California

Cooking OIL
1 ONION (chopped)
1 lb. GROUND BEEF
½ GREEN PEPPER (chopped)
1 can (#2½) TOMATOES
2 cans (#303) KIDNEY BEANS
½ cup WATER
3 Tbsp. FLOUR
2 or 3 Fresh CHILI PEPPERS
¼ tsp. GARLIC POWDER
½ tsp. CUMIN
1 tsp. OREGANO
1 tsp. SOY SAUCE
2 tsp. CHILI POWDER
2 tsp. BROWN SUGAR
1 Tbsp. SALT

Brown onion, meat and green pepper. Add tomatoes and beans. In a blender, combine water, flour and chili peppers. Blend until peppers are chopped well, adding to chili with remaining ingredients and simmer 30 minutes more. (Serves 4)

For Those Who Like It Hot

Ruth Grant -- Santa Cruz, California

1 lb. RED BEANS
4 Tbsp. OIL
4 ONIONS (chopped)
2 lbs. GROUND BEEF
2 cans (28-oz.) TOMATOES
1½ Tbsp. SALT
1 tsp. PEPPER
3 Tbsp. CHILI POWDER
5 Tbsp. CUMIN
6 whole CHILETEPINS
    (crushed)

Rinse beans and soak overnight. Drain bean water, add fresh water to cover, plus one inch, in large pan and cook until tender. Pour oil into heated skillet and saute onions until tender. Add onions to cooked beans. Brown ground beef and add to beans. Add remaining ingredients to beans and cook half an hour. (For less "hot" chili, use fewer chiletepins.) (Serves 8 to 10)

Old-Fashioned Chili

Mrs. Ralph Brown -- Los Baños, California

2 lbs. MEAT (chili ground)
2 med. ONIONS (chopped)
1 clove GARLIC (chopped)
1 can (14½-oz.) TOMATOES
    (undrained)
3 Tbsp. CHILI POWDER
Dash RED PEPPER
SALT to taste
1 can (6-oz.) TOMATO PASTE
2 cups cooked PINTO BEANS

Brown beef with onion and garlic. Pour off grease. Add tomatoes, chili powder, red pepper and salt. Simmer one hour. Add tomato paste mixed with water. Simmer another hour, stirring often. Stir in cooked pinto beans. (Serves 8)

L & P's Old-Fashioned Chili

Paula Roe -- Mesa, Arizona

1 lb. lean GROUND BEEF
1 can (16-oz.) Red Kidney BEANS
¼ cup ONION (chopped)
1 can (4-oz.) TOMATO PASTE
1 Tbsp. CHILI POWDER
1 can (27-oz.) peeled TOMATOES
6 Hot Pickled PEPPERS
3½ to 4 cups WATER

In a skillet, brown ground beef and drain excess fat. In a 5-quart saucepan, combine ground beef, kidney beans, onion, tomato paste and chili powder. Add liquid from tomatoes. Cut peeled tomatoes in halves. Remove stems from pickled peppers, cut in halves. Add to other ingredients with tomatoes. Add water and simmer four hours, stirring occasionally. (Serves 4)

All-American Chili

Courtesy McIlhenny Co., mfrs. TABASCO Brand Pepper Sauce

2 lbs. GROUND BEEF
1 lg. ONION (chopped)
2 cloves GARLIC (minced)
3 to 5 Tbsp. CHILI POWDER
1 tsp. SALT
1 tsp. dried leaf OREGANO
1 to 2 tsp. TABASCO Pepper
   Sauce
1 can (16-oz.) TOMATOES
1 can (8-oz.) TOMATO SAUCE
1 cup WATER
2 cans (16-oz.) Red KIDNEY
   BEANS (drained)

In large saucepan, break up ground beef. Add onion and garlic; cook, stirring frequently, until beef is browned and vegetables are tender. Add remaining ingredients and mix well. Bring to a boil; reduce heat. Simmer, uncovered, 45 minutes (or until thickened), stirring occasionally. (Serves 6 to 8)

Trueheart Chili (Low-Sodium)

Margaret M. Edmister -- San Rafael, California

1 lb. DRY BEANS
2 to 3 Tbsp. Vegetable OIL
FLOUR to dredge meat
1 lb. BEEF HEART
1 lb. lean BEEF CHUCK
1 lg. ONION (chopped)
2 lg. cloves GARLIC (minced)
1 cup CELERY (diced)
2 Tbsp. CHILI POWDER
1 tsp. TURMERIC
1 tsp. MARJORAM
1 Tbsp. Instant DECAF Coffee
½ tsp. NUTMEG
½ tsp. OREGANO
1 can (10½-oz.) TOMATO PUREE

Soak beans overnight. Next morning, simmer beans in bean liquid and one tablespoon oil until almost tender. (Use minimum water, adding some during cooking.)

Have meats semi-frozen to cut into 1/2'' to 1'' cubes. Dredge meat cubes with minimum of flour. Heat remaining oil in skillet and saute meat to brown, adding onion, garlic and celery. Add remaining ingredients to skillet and simmer about an hour. Combine meat and beans and simmer about 40 to 50 minutes. To thicken, mash beans against side of pan. (Serves 6 to 8)

Carol's Quick Chili

Carol Stinnett -- Middle Point, Ohio

1 lb. HAMBURGER
1 cup ONION (chopped)
1 can (15-oz.) KIDNEY BEANS
1 can (8-oz.) TOMATO SAUCE
1/8 tsp. CAYENNE
2 Tbsp. Hot TACO SAUCE
¾ tsp. SALT
2 JALAPENO PEPPERS (optional)

Brown hamburger and onion in large iron skillet. Add kidney beans (drained), and remaining ingredients. Cover; simmer 1 to 1 1/2 hours. (If using fresh jalapeno peppers, remove seeds. Also, OMIT cayenne and hot taco sauce. For a milder chili, use only one jalapeno.) (Serves 4)

Zesty Chili

Jim H. De Vault -- Rancho Cordova, California

1 lg. ONION (chopped)
¼ cup MARGARINE
1½ lbs. GROUND BEEF
3 Tbsp. CHILI POWDER
¼ tsp. GARLIC POWDER
½ tsp. CORIANDER (ground)
1 tsp. CUMIN POWDER
2 small Red CHILI PEPPERS
   (crushed)
2 BAY LEAVES
½ tsp. SALT
¼ tsp. PEPPER
1 can (30-oz.) RED BEANS
1 can (28-oz.) whole TOMATOES
3 Tbsp. FLOUR
¼ cup cold WATER

Cook onion in margarine until soft, and set aside. Brown meat until light brown in color. Drain excess fat. Add onions, spices and beans to browned meat. Drain and mash tomatoes with wire potato masher and add to meat mixture. Mix flour with cold water and add to chili as a thickener. Simmer on low heat one to two hours. (Serves 6 to 8)

Chili Rojo

Courtesy Heublein -- Grocery Products Group

1 lb. lean BEEF CHUCK (½" cubes)
1 Tbsp. OIL
1 med. clove GARLIC (minced)
1 med. ONION (sliced)
1 can (6-oz.) TOMATO PASTE
1 tsp. SALT
1 Tbsp. PAPRIKA
1 can (7-oz.) Ortega Diced GREEN
   CHILES
1 can (10½-oz.) condensed
   ONION SOUP
1 can (16-oz.) PINTO BEANS
¼ tsp. ground CUMIN
1 cup WATER

In large skillet, brown beef in oil. Stir in remaining ingredients. Simmer, covered, 1 1/2 hours. (Serves 4 to 6)

Wisconsin Chili

Joan von Germeten -- Paradise Valley, Arizona

1 can (28-oz.) whole TOMATOES
1½ cups TOMATO JUICE
½ tsp. BAKING SODA
1 Tbsp. MARGARINE
1½ cups ONIONS (sliced thin)
¼ tsp. SALT
1 lb. GROUND CHUCK
1 can (15½-oz.) Red KIDNEY
  BEANS
¼ cup CELERY (chopped fine)
1 tsp. SALT
1 tsp. SUGAR
1½ tsp. CHILI POWDER
¼ tsp. PEPPER

Put tomatoes and tomato juice in a large pot and bring to a boil. Add baking soda and turn heat off. Melt margarine in frypan and brown onions. Sprinkle onions with 1/4 teaspoon salt. Put onions into tomato mixture. In the same frypan, brown meat slightly and pour off grease. Put browned meat into tomato-onion mixture. Add beans (slightly drained) and remaining ingredients and stir. Simmer about two hours, stirring occasionally. (Serves 4 to 6)

Chili a la Super Creole

Clara Moreland -- Oakland, California

6 Tbsp. BUTTER
5 med. ONIONS (sliced)
3 lbs. GROUND BEEF
2 Tbsp. CHILI POWDER
1 Tbsp. SALT
1 tsp. PAPRIKA
¾ tsp. TABASCO
3 cans (16-oz.) TOMATOES
1 can (8-oz.) TOMATO SAUCE
1 can (6-oz.) TOMATO PASTE
3 cans (20-oz.) KIDNEY BEANS

Melt butter in a 6-to-8-quart saucepan. Add onion and cook until tender, but not brown. Add ground beef; sprinkle with chili powder, salt, paprika and Tabasco. Cook meat until brown, breaking up with a fork. Add tomatoes, tomato sauce and tomato paste. Cover; simmer 45 minutes. Add beans and simmer 15 minutes longer. (Serves 12)

Lima Chili

Courtesy Gebhardt's Mexican Foods -- San Antonio, Texas

1 cup Dry BABY LIMA BEANS
3 cups boiling WATER
2 strips BACON
¼ cup ONION (chopped)
1 cup CELERY (coarsely chopped)
1 clove GARLIC
½ lb. chopped BEEF
2 Tbsp. FLOUR
1 tsp. Gebhardt's CHILI POWDER
½ tsp. SALT
Dashes PEPPER
½ cup WATER
1 can (6-oz.) TOMATO PASTE

Put lima beans into boiling water. Cover and simmer two hours or more. At the end of cooking time, place strips of bacon in a large skillet and fry until nearly crisp. Remove bacon from pan and lightly brown the chopped onion, celery and garlic clove in the hot bacon fat.

Remove the clove of garlic and discard. Push vegetables to one side of the pan and break off bits of the ground beef into the pan. Cook beef pieces until browned well.

Combine flour, chili powder, sugar, salt, pepper and water to form a smooth paste. Blend in the tomato paste and add to the cooked meat and vegetables, stirring to form a thick gravy consistency.

Add undrained lima beans and stir the mixture a few times. Cover and simmer over very low heat for an hour or until beans are tender. (Add water from time to time if mixture becomes too dry.) (Serves 4 to 6)

Main-Dish Chili

Lou Ann Houser -- San Jose, California

1 Tbsp. BUTTER
1 ONION (chopped)
½ cup CELERY (chopped)
1 GREEN PEPPER (cut up)
1 lb. GROUND BEEF

1 tsp. SALT
¼ tsp. CHILI POWDER
1 can (#303) KIDNEY BEANS
1 can (8-oz.) TOMATO SAUCE
2 Tbsp. uncooked RICE
1 can (10¾-oz.) TOMATO SOUP

Melt shortening in pan. Add onion, celery, and green pepper and fry until golden brown. Add meat, salt and chili powder and simmer until meat loses color. Add remaining ingredients and cook slowly on low heat for 45 minutes. (Serves 6 to 8)

Chili con Carne Soup

Norma Jean Coppenbarger -- Sacramento, California

2 Tbsp. SALAD OIL
1 med GREEN PEPPER
1 small ONION
1 clove GARLIC (minced)
1 cup CELERY (chopped)
1 lb. GROUND CHUCK
1 tsp. SALT
1 tsp. SUGAR
1 can (12-oz.) TOMATO PASTE
3 cans (12-oz.) WATER
1 can (16-oz.) TOMATOES
1½ Tbsp. CHILI POWDER
1 can (16-oz.) Red KIDNEY BEANS
CHEDDAR CHEESE

Chop green pepper; slice onion thinly. Heat oil in a large pot and saute green pepper, onion, garlic and celery until tender (about five minutes). Add meat and cook, uncovered, until meat is brown. Add remaining ingredients (EXCEPT beans and cheese). Cover and simmer 45 minutes. Add beans and simmer, uncovered, 15 minutes. Serve with grated cheese. (Serves 6)

Penny-Pincher's Chili

Joellen Crouch -- Corte Madera, California

1 lb. GROUND BEEF
1 lg. ONION (chopped)
3 Tbsp. CHILI POWDER
1 tsp. SALT
1 tsp. PEPPER
1 tsp. GARLIC POWDER
½ tsp. CAYENNE POWDER
1 can (15-oz.) TOMATO SAUCE
1 can (16-oz.) stewed TOMATOES
1 can (15-oz.) Red KIDNEY BEANS
2 cups WATER
1 cup Elbow MACARONI

Brown ground beef and add onion. Cook until tender and add all seasonings. Stir to blend well. Add tomato sauce, stewed tomatoes and beans. Simmer over medium heat for 30 minutes, stirring occasionally. Add water and continue to simmer 30 minutes more.

Cook macaroni separately until tender, and add to chili 15 minutes before serving. (Serves 6 to 8)

Truck Stop Chili #2

Barbara Lowder -- Phoenix, Arizona

1 can (#303) Hunts TOMATOES
1 can (6-oz.) TOMATO PASTE
1 tsp. SALT
1 tsp. PEPPER
2 tsp. CHILI POWDER
1 lg. ONION
1 small GREEN PEPPER
1½ lbs. Top Round STEAK
1 pkg. (6-oz.) Jimmy Dean
    SAUSAGE LINKS
1 can (#303) small RED BEANS
1 can (8-oz.) GARBANZO BEANS
(drained)

Put tomatoes into large saucepan and break into pieces with a fork. Add tomato paste, salt, pepper and chili powder and start mixture to simmer. Chop onion and green pepper and saute in a skillet. Push to one side of skillet. Cut round steak and sausage links into bite-size pieces and brown in same skillet. Put onion, pepper and meat into saucepan with tomatoes, cover, and simmer about two hours. Add beans before serving and heat thoroughly. (Serves 4)

West Texas Chili

Eva L. McDowell -- Sun City, Arizona

1 Tbsp. Vegetable OIL
2 lg. ONIONS
½ cup GREEN PEPPER
1 cup CELERY
2 lbs. HAMBURGER
1 Tbsp. SALT
1 tsp. BLACK PEPPER
2 Tbsp. CHILI POWDER
1 tsp. SUGAR
3 small CHILI PEPPERS (dried)
1 can (46-oz.) TOMATO JUICE
2 med. cans CHILI BEANS

Chop onions, green pepper and celery (stalk and leaves) very fine. Saute in oil, stirring frequently. Place sauteed vegetables in kettle in which chili will be simmered. Add meat to saute pan and brown, adding salt, pepper, chili powder and sugar. Crush chili peppers and sprinkle over meat. Add seasoned meat to vegetables. Add tomato juice (and water, if desired), and simmer one hour. Add beans, simmer several hours. (Serves 10)

Mel's Chili

(Created by Judy Pierce)

2 lbs. lean GROUND BEEF
1 ONION (chopped)
2 cans (6-oz.) TOMATO
    PASTE
6 cans (6-oz.) WATER
1 clove GARLIC (mashed)
SALT & PEPPER
1 can (30-oz.) CHILI BEANS
2 pkg. Lawry's CHILI
    Seasoning MIX

Vic Tayback -- "MEL"

Brown meat, add onion and saute until tender. Stir in tomato paste, water, and garlic. Simmer until thick--about two hours. Add remaining ingredients and cook about 15 minutes longer. Serve as is, or over spaghetti, topped with cheese. (Serves 6).

Maria's Chili Beans

Maria Bloeser -- Corte Madera, California

2 lbs. Cranberry BEANS
1 Tbsp. Cooking OIL
1 cup ONIONS
2 lg. cloves GARLIC
1 cup GREEN PEPPERS
2 lbs. GROUND BEEF
2 Tbsp. VINEGAR
4 Tbsp. CHILI POWDER
½ tsp. CAYENNE
4 tsp. SALT

Fresh Ground PEPPER
2 BAY LEAVES
½ bunch PARSLEY (chopped fine)
1 Tbsp. OREGANO

Pinches: Sugar, Marjoram, Sweet
    Basil, Ground Cumin, Celery Seed
4 cups TOMATOES
2 cans (8-oz.) TOMATO SAUCE
1 can (6-oz.) TOMATO PASTE

Wash cranberry beans (or other beans); cover with water and bring to a boil. Let boil two minutes. Turn off fire and let stand in hot water one hour. Then proceed cooking beans until tender but whole. Mince onions, green pepper and garlic. Heat oil in frypan and saute beef, onions, garlic and green peppers.

Add remaining ingredients EXCEPT tomatoes, tomato sauce, tomato paste and beans. Simmer meat 10 minutes.

Put tomatoes (canned or fresh) through a blender at puree speed (one cup at a time). If using canned tomatoes, include juice. Turn meat into heavy pot or Dutch oven. Add pureed tomatoes, tomato sauce and tomato paste. (Paste should be well mashed into sauce.) Bring to a boil and simmer 1/2 hour.

Drain beans (save cooking water); add beans to meat. Simmer two hours; taste and correct seasoning after first hour. If mixture is too thick, add juice from cooked beans. For extra zest, add a couple of beef bouillon cubes. (Serves 8 to 10)

Mescalero Chili

Barbara I. Wagner -- Watsonville, California

3 lb. CHUCK ROAST
2-3 lb. HAM BUTT
1½ lb. GROUND BEEF
½ lb. Italian SAUSAGE
1 lb. BEANS
1 ONION
2 cloves GARLIC
1 BELL PEPPER
2 JALAPENO PEPPERS
1 can (15-oz.) TOMATO SAUCE
1 can (16-oz) stewed TOMATOES
SALT and PEPPER to taste

In Dutch oven or large pan, add roast, ham butt, ground beef and sausage with water to cover the meats. Bring to a boil. While meats are cooking, soak beans in large bowl til beans swell in size; set aside.

Chop onion, garlic, green pepper and add to boiling mixture with tomato sauce and stewed tomatoes. Simmer til meat falls away from bone.

Add beans and part of water they've soaked in. Simmer til beans are tender (24 hours in a crock pot set on medium setting). Transfer to a 2 1/2 quart baking dish, sprinkle with grated cheese, and bake in a 325 F oven about 20 minutes. (Serves 6 to 10)

Lorene's Texas Chili

Lorene Dunn -- Wichita Falls, Texas

4 Tbsp. BACON GREASE
2 lg. ONIONS (chopped)
6 cloves GARLIC (chopped)
SALT to taste
2 lbs. GROUND BEEF
3 Tbsp. CHILI POWDER
2 cans (#2) TOMATOES
1 can (#2) Red KIDNEY BEANS
2 Tbsp. COMINO SEEDS
(tied in a bag)

Heat bacon grease in a skillet. Add onions and garlic and cook until tender, but not brown. Mix meat with salt and chili powder and add to onions. Cook until meat is done. Then, add tomatoes, beans and comino seed. Simmer, covered, for about two hours. (Makes two quarts)

Fiesta Chili

Joseph T. Wanner -- Fairfield, California

8 slices BACON
1 lb. Italian SAUSAGE
1 lb. Ground CHUCK
2 med. ONIONS
4 GREEN ONIONS
4 cloves GARLIC
2 cans (8-oz.) TOMATO SAUCE
1 can (28-oz.) TOMATOES
2 cans (15-oz.) KIDNEY BEANS
2 CHILI PEPPERS
2 tsp. CUMIN
2 tsp. OREGANO
2 tsp. BASIL
SALT to taste

Slice the sausage. Chop onions and chili peppers very fine. Crush garlic cloves. Cut up canned tomatoes. Fry bacon until crisp; set strips aside. Drain all but one tablespoon bacon drippings and fry Italian sausage, ground chuck, onions and garlic until brown. Drain. Crumble bacon and add to ground chuck mixture along with remaining ingredients. Simmer for 30 minutes. (Serves 6 to 8)

Bueno Chili con Carne

Jean B. Bailey -- Tucson, Arizona

2 Tbsp. Vegetable OIL
3 med. ONIONS
2 med. GREEN PEPPERS
1 can (4-oz.) diced GREEN
  CHILES
2 Tbsp. CHILI POWDER
2 Tbsp. CUMIN
SALT and PEPPER to taste
3 lbs. GROUND BEEF
3 cans (15-oz.) Dark Red
  KIDNEY BEANS
2 cans (28-oz.) Italian Style
  TOMATOES

Chop onions and green peppers fine. Heat oil in a skillet and saute onions, peppers, chiles, chili powder, cumin, salt and pepper. Add ground beef and brown. Add kidney beans and tomatoes to browned meat. Cover pan and simmer, stirring mixture occasionally. Simmer eight hours. (Serves 8)

Carmen's Mexican Chili with Beans

Carmen L. Garcia -- Santa Clara, California

2 cups PINTO BEANS
7 cups WATER
2 tsp. SALT
1 lb. GROUND BEEF
½ lb. BEEF CHORIZO
1 clove GARLIC
½ cup ONION
½ cup CELERY
1 Tbsp. Gebhardt's CHILI
   POWDER
3 Tbsp. FLOUR

Wash beans. Cook in 7 cups of water over low heat for 2 1/2 hours. Add salt, cook 30 minutes more.

Chop onion and garlic fine; slice celery fine and dice. Fry ground meat in skillet. Drain. Add chorizo (Mexican sausage), fry until it separates. Add garlic, onions, celery and chili powder. Stir-fry for one minute; add flour and stir-fry for another minute. Put meat mixture into beans and simmer for thirty minutes. Stir occasionally. (Serves 10 to 12)

Chili a la Toepfer

Mary Beccio -- San Rafael, California

1 lb. KIDNEY BEANS
10 cups cold WATER
1 Tbsp. BUTTER
2 lbs. GROUND CHUCK
2 lg. ONIONS (chopped)
2 lg. GREEN PEPPERS (chopped)
2 Tbsp. CHILI POWDER
2 Tbsp. Red Wine GARLIC
   VINEGAR
1 Tbsp. SALT
½ tsp. GARLIC POWDER
1 can (46-oz.) TOMATO JUICE

Soak beans overnight. Pour off water in morning and rinse. Put beans in large pot, add cold water, bring to a boil, and boil slowly for 1 1/2 hours, stirring often. Melt butter in a skillet, and add meat, sauteing for 10 minutes. (Break meat with a fork while sauteing.) Combine remaining ingredients (EXCEPT tomato juice) with meat and stir. Add meat mixture to beans and cover with tomato juice. Cook two hours more, until thick. (Serves 8)

Lynne's Special Chili

Lynne S. Rose -- Phoenix, Arizona

3 to 4 lbs. BEEF BRISKET
¼ cup OIL
4 ONIONS (chopped)
2 cloves GARLIC
1 can BEEF BROTH
2 cans (16-oz.) TOMATO SAUCE
2 cans (16-oz.) PINTO BEANS
1 can (7-oz.) diced GREEN
    CHILES
1½ tsp. SALT
¾ tsp. PEPPER
3 Tbsp. CHILI POWDER
CAYENNE to taste
¼ cup MASA HARINA
¾ cup WATER

Cut beef brisket into bite-size pieces. Brown beef in oil. Add garlic and onions and cook until onions curl. Add beef broth, tomato sauce, beans, chiles, and seasonings. Simmer from 4 to 5 hours.

Mix water and Masa Harina in a jar and shake very well. Add, as needed, to thicken chili, stirring constantly. Simmer 15 minutes more. (Serves 10)

Bonnie's Chili

Bonnie Brown -- San Jose, California

1 lb. GROUND BEEF
1 lg. ONION (chopped)
1 clove GARLIC (minced)
2 tsp. SALT
¼ tsp. PAPRIKA
½ to 1 tsp. ground CUMIN
1 Tbsp. OREGANO
2 to 3 Tbsp. CHILI POWDER
1/8 tsp. CAYENNE
1 can (8-oz.) TOMATO SAUCE
1 can (16-oz.) stewed TOMATOES
2 cans (16-oz.) KIDNEY BEANS
    (drained)

Brown beef, onions and garlic in oil. Drain grease and add remaining ingredients. Cover, simmer 30 minutes. (Serves 4)

Mama's Three-Bean Chili

Jeanette Boettcher -- Saratoga, California

2 Tbsp. SALAD OIL
½ lb. POLISH SAUSAGE
1½ lb. GROUND BEEF
1 med. ONION (chopped)
1 lg. clove GARLIC (minced)
1 can (16-oz.) whole TOMATOES
1 can (27-oz.) KIDNEY BEANS
1 can (16-oz.) PORK & BEANS
1 can (17-oz.) REFRIED BEANS
1 can (4-oz) chopped GREEN
   CHILES
1 can (8-oz.) TOMATO SAUCE
1½ tsp. SALT
¼ tsp. BLACK PEPPER
1 tsp. CUMIN (ground)
2 to 4 tsp. ground CHILI
   POWDER
1 tsp. leaf OREGANO (crushed)
2/3 cup JACK CHEESE

Mince sausage. Heat salad oil in a 5-to-6-quart Dutch oven. Add beef and minced sausage and cook until meat is brown and crumbly. Add onion and garlic and cook until onion is transparent, stirring occasionally. Pour off accumulated fat. Add tomatoes (undrained and coarsely chopped), kidney beans (undrained), pork and beans (undrained), green chiles (drained), and remaining ingredients EXCEPT cheese, stirring well to combine. Bring to a boil; simmer, uncovered, over low heat for two to three hours, stirring to prevent sticking. Serve in bowls and sprinkle with shredded cheese. (Serves 10)

Best Ever One-Pan Chili

Helen (Mrs. Robert) Wisener -- Middle Point, Ohio

1 lb. HAMBURGER
1 can (46-oz.) TOMATO JUICE
1 lg. ONION (chopped)
1 Tbsp. SALT
½ tsp. CHILI POWDER
1 can (#2) Light KIDNEY BEANS

Mix hamburger and tomato juice with hands. Add onion, salt, chili powder and beans and mix again. Put mixture into large, heavy pot and simmer two hours. (Serves 4 to 6)

Dan's Favorite Chili

Dan Mathews -- Los Gatos, California

1½ lbs. HAMBURGER
½ ONION (chopped)
1 can (15-oz.) TOMATO SAUCE
1 can (16-oz.) KIDNEY BEANS
2 tsp. CHILI POWDER
1 Tbsp. FLOUR
3 Tbsp. WATER
1 tsp. SALT

Brown hamburger and chopped onion in large skillet. Add tomato sauce and kidney beans. Combine remaining ingredients and mix until smooth. Add to skillet, stir well and simmer for 10 minutes. (Serves 4 to 6)

Chilly-Time Chili

Joan Greene -- La Canada, California

Wesson OIL
1 med. ONION (diced)
1½ lbs. ROUND STEAK
SALT and PEPPER
3 cans (16-oz.) Van Camp Dark Red
   KIDNEY BEANS
1 can (8-oz.) TOMATO SAUCE
1½ Tbsp. Gebhardt's CHILI
   POWDER
1 cup WATER

Have meat ground twice. Heat oil in a large skillet and saute onion. Add meat, salt and pepper and brown. Add undrained beans, tomato sauce and chili powder. Rinse cans with water and add to chili. Bring to almost boiling. Turn down heat and simmer 20 minutes. (Serves 4)

Old-Fashioned Northern Chili

Helen M. Eisenmann -- Yuma, Arizona

1 lb. GROUND BEEF
½ cup WATER
1 tsp. SALT
1½ tsp. CHILI POWDER
1 can (15-oz.) TOMATO SAUCE
2 cans (15-oz.) RED BEANS

Place beef, water, salt and chili powder in a deep pan and simmer 1/2 hour (or until beef is tender). Stir in tomato sauce and beans and simmer 30 minutes longer. (Serves 4)

Kika's Chili Beans

Congressman Kika de la Garza -- 15th District, Texas

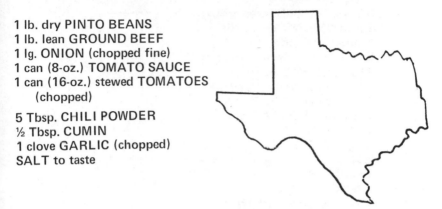

1 lb. dry PINTO BEANS
1 lb. lean GROUND BEEF
1 lg. ONION (chopped fine)
1 can (8-oz.) TOMATO SAUCE
1 can (16-oz.) stewed TOMATOES
    (chopped)

5 Tbsp. CHILI POWDER
½ Tbsp. CUMIN
1 clove GARLIC (chopped)
SALT to taste

Clean and wash beans. Place in a large pot and cover with cold water. Let soak overnight. Next day, heat to boiling, reduce heat and simmer for 30 minutes. Brown meat in a frypan and drain. Add other ingredients to meat, mix, then add to beans and cook until beans are tender (about one hour). Stir often.   (Serves 6 to 8)

Chili Supreme

Bill Siren -- Sunnyvale, California

3 cloves GARLIC (minced)
2 Tbsp. Vegetable OIL
3 lbs. ROUND STEAK (coarse)
1 lg. ONION (chopped)
1 lg. GREEN PEPPER (chopped)
1 stalk CELERY (chopped)
3 cans (16-oz.) Red KIDNEY
    BEANS (drained)

1 can (6-oz.) TOMATO PASTE
1 can (16-oz.) stewed TOMATOES
2 cans (15-oz.) TOMATO SAUCE

4 tsp. CHILI POWDER
4 BAY LEAVES
1 Tbsp. SALT
1 Hot GREEN CHILI (2")
1-oz. CHILI SALSA
1 dash CAYENNE
1 dash OREGANO
12-oz. BEER
½ cup MASA HARINA
1 dash GARLIC SALT
1 dash coarse ground PEPPER

Heat oil in skillet and cook garlic until golden. Add meat and brown evenly.   Pour off some oil into another skillet and cook onions, pepper and celery until tender. Combine all ingredients in a large pan, cover, and cook over low heat for two hours. (Serves 12)

Mrs. Tom Bradley's Chili

Ethel (Mrs. Tom) Bradley -- Los Angeles, California

3 Tbsp. OIL (safflower or soy)
2 med ONIONS (chopped)
1 clove GARLIC (minced)
2 GREEN PEPPERS (chopped)
2 lbs. GROUND ROUND
4 to 6 Tbsp. CHILI POWDER
2 cans Whole TOMATOES
1 can (6-oz.) TOMATO SAUCE
1½ tsp. SALT
½ tsp. PEPPER
2 CLOVES
1 BAY LEAF
¼ tsp. PAPRIKA
1 Tbsp. Ground CUMIN
2 cans (20-oz.) KIDNEY BEANS (drained)

In cooking oil, saute finely chopped onions, garlic, and green peppers. Add ground beef and brown, mixing thoroughly, so that meat is crumbled. Add some of the chile powder while these ingredients are browning.

In a large pot, simmer the tomatoes, tomato sauce and spices. When meat is thoroughly browned and crumbled, add meat, onions, and green pepper to the other ingredients in the large pot. Add canned chili beans. (Serves 4 to 6)

Chili Casa de Doris

Doris E. Craig -- Kingman, Arizona

1 lb. GROUND ROUND
2 oz. MARGARINE
1 Tbsp. Wesson OIL
2 med. ONIONS (chopped)
2 cloves GARLIC (chopped fine)
2 cans (15-oz.) KIDNEY BEANS
2 cans (16-oz.) whole TOMATOES
2 Tbsp. CHILI POWDER
SALT to taste

Place meat in a 4-to-6-quart pot and panfry until it begins to brown. In a small skillet, heat margarine and oil and fry onion and garlic until soft. Add onions and garlic with remaining ingredients to meat. Simmer, covered, 30 minutes. (Serves 6)

Spitfire Chili

Frances M. Stoskus -- Baldwin Park, California

1 lb. PINTO BEANS
1 small jar SMALL COCKTAIL ONIONS
½ lb. SLAB BACON (1" cubes)
¾ tsp. THYME
1¼ tsp. toasted CUMIN
4 Tbsp. pure CHILI POWDER
1½ cups TOMATO PASTE
1½ cups canned Pear-Shaped Italian
TOMATOES
2 Tbsp. LIQUID (from cocktail
onions)
¼ cup VODKA
3 Tbsp. fresh LIME JUICE
1 Tbsp. SUGAR
1 tsp. SALT
½ tsp. SEASONED PEPPER

Soak beans overnight. Drain. Add fresh water to cover. Add liquid from onions (reserving the two tablespoons). Bring to a boil and cook until just tender. Drain and set aside. Saute bacon cubes in skillet and remove from skillet. Add small onions, thyme, cumin, chili powder, tomato paste, tomatoes and two tablespoons onion liquid in skillet and heat thoroughly. Blend with beans. Place in baking dish.

Pour vodka and lime juice over all. (One Vodka Gimlet may be used in lieu of vodka and lime juice.) Sprinkle sugar, salt and seasoned pepper on top. Place sauted bacon cubes on mixture. Cover dish and bake one hour in preheated 350 oven. More liquid may be added. (Serves 6 to 8)

Arizona Trail Chili

Ed Karn -- Green Valley, Arizona

1 lb. GROUND CHUCK
2 cans (15-oz.) PINTO BEANS
1-oz. ground CUMIN
2-oz. CHILI POWDER
½-oz. ground CHILI PEPPER

Combine pinto beans with ground cumin, chili powder and ground chili pepper in a heavy pot and simmer, stirring so all ingredients are mixed completely. Panfry meat in skillet until almost cooked through. Add meat to beanpot, and simmer for one hour, stirring every 15 minutes. (Serves 2 to 4)

Company Chili

Sue DeRoy -- Salinas, California

2 Tbsp. BACON FAT
1 cup ONION (diced)
½ cup GREEN PEPPER (diced)
½ lb. GROUND ROUND (coarse)
½ lb. GROUND LAMB
1 lb. BEEF CHORIZO
1 can (32-oz.) stewed TOMATOES
½ tsp. CUMIN
½ tsp. SALT
1 tsp. SUGAR
1 can (8-oz.) TOMATO SAUCE
2 cups KIDNEY BEANS
1 cup JACK CHEESE

In a large skillet, heat bacon fat and saute diced onions and peppers until tender. Add beef and lamb. Brown meat and drain all fat. Add chorizo and cook down (DO NOT drain). Turn heat to simmer and add tomatoes, cumin, salt, sugar, and tomato sauce. Simmer for one hour, covered. Uncover and simmer another 40 minutes. (Add water if mixture is too thick.) Stir in beans (undrained) and heat to boiling point. Serve with sprinkling of shredded cheese. (Serves 4 to 6)

Donna's Chili

Donna L. Van Houten -- Phoenix, Arizona

2 lbs. lean GROUND BEEF
2 lg. ONIONS (chopped fine)
1 tsp. GARLIC POWDER
1 Green BELL PEPPER (chopped)
1 Tbsp. CHILI POWDER
2 cartons Baca's Red CHILI BASE
1/3 cup SUGAR
2 cans (16-oz.) small RED BEANS
2 cans (16-oz.) Peeled TOMATOES
1 can (32-oz.) TOMATO SAUCE
2 quarts WATER

Combine meat, onions, garlic powder and bell pepper and brown. Drain off all fat. Add remaining ingredients and bring to a boil. Simmer slowly 4 to 6 hours. (Serves 8)

For crock pot cooking, follow above instructions, but add only 8 oz. water. Cook on low heat from 8 to 10 hours.

(Recipe may be increased by doubling all ingredients EXCEPT chili base and chili powder. Add only one block of chili base for each extra batch; use chili powder to taste.)

Sombrero Chili

Irene Elliott -- Turlock, California

2 lbs. lean CHUCK (1" cubes)
¼ cup sifted FLOUR
2 Tbsp. CHILI POWDER
2 tsp. SALT
¼ tsp. PEPPER
¼ cup SHORTENING
1 lg. ONION (chopped)
2 cans (16-oz.) Red KIDNEY
   BEANS
2 cans (16-oz.) TOMATOES
1 can (16-oz.) Whole Kernel CORN
2 Tbsp. BUTTER
2 cups cooked RICE
4-oz. CHEDDAR CHEESE
1 can (4-oz.) PIMIENTOS
1 can (3-oz.) Hot CHILI PEPPERS

In a paper bag, shake beef cubes with flour, chili powder, salt and pepper to coat well. Brown (a few cubes at a time) in shortening (or bacon drippings) in a Dutch oven. Return all meat to kettle. Stir in onion and saute until onions are soft. Spoon off excess drippings; stir remaining flour seasoning mixture into pan.

Drain liquid from kidney beans and add to meat; stir in tomatoes, cover. Simmer, stirring several times, for 11/2 hours Stir in kidney beans, heat just to boiling.

To serve, drain corn and heat in butter in small saucepan. Spoon hot chili into heated 12-cup serving bowl. Spoon corn in a layer in center; top with a cone of hot cooked rice. Sprinkle with grated cheese, pimentos and chili peppers. (Serves 8)

Catoctin Chili

Rebecca F. (Mrs. George) Gaffney -- Richardson, Texas

1½ lbs. GROUND BEEF
1 med. ONION
1 med. GREEN PEPPER
3 stalks CELERY

1 tsp. SALT
¼ tsp. PEPPER
2½ Tbsp. CHILI POWDER
1 can (16-oz.) TOMATOES
1 can (16-oz.) KIDNEY BEANS

Chop onion, green pepper and celery. Brown ground beef and chopped onion. Add green pepper and celery and cook 10 minutes. Add seasonings and tomatoes and simmer about 2 hours. Add beans and cook 15 minutes more. (Serves 5)

Crows Nest Chili Beans

William (Bill) M. Crowston -- Sacramento, California

4½ cups PINK BEANS
2 tsp. SALT
4 med. ONIONS
1 lb. GROUND ROUND
2½ lbs. GROUND BEEF
3 cans (2 lbs.) whole TOMATOES
4 tsp. SALT
Dash PAPRIKA
½ tsp. CAYENNE
2 BAY LEAVES
6 Tbsp. CHILI POWDER
4 cloves GARLIC (crushed)
¼ tsp. BLACK PEPPER
1 tsp. OREGANO
2 pinches CUMIN
2 Tbsp. SUGAR

In a 10-quart pot, cover beans wih water, add salt and bring
to a boil (uncovered) for three minutes. Cover, remove from
heat, allowing beans to soak for 10 hours. Drain; separate beans
from liquid in separate containers and save both for later use.

Chop onions fine, combine with meat in frypan, brown, and
set aside.

Combine remaining ingredients with browned meat in 10-quart
pot, cover, and simmer two hours. Add drained beans and simmer
1 1/2 hours. (Drained bean liquid may be added periodically for
desired consistency.) (Serves 20-24)

Ruth's Chili

Ruth (Mrs. W. M.) Kolstad -- Apache Junction, Arizona

2½ cups PINTO BEANS
6 cups WATER
1 tsp. SALT
4 Tbsp. BUTTER
2 lbs. GROUND BEEF

1 Tbsp. Lawry's SEASONED
SALT
1 can (16-oz.) TOMATOES
1 can (28-oz.) TOMATOES
3 Tbsp. Gebhardt's CHILI
POWDER

Wash beans; soak overnight in water and salt. Next morning,
cook beans about four hours (until tender), and mash. Sprinkle
Lawry's Seasoned Salt over meat and mix well. Heat butter
in skillet and saute meat. Break up tomatoes and put into
large, heavy pot. Add meat, mashed beans and chili powder.
Simmer for about four hours. (Serves 12)

Dorothy's Tasty Chili

Dorothy Maxwell -- Sacramento, California

2 lbs. GROUND BEEF
1 ONION (chopped)
1 clove GARLIC (crushed)
1 GREEN PEPPER (chopped)
½ cup CELERY (chopped)
1 can (28-oz.) TOMATOES
2 cups TOMATO JUICE
2 Tbsp. CHILI POWDER
1 Tbsp. SUGAR
2 tsp. SALT
1 BAY LEAF
½ tsp. OREGANO
2 cans (16-oz.) Red KIDNEY BEANS (drained)

With a fork, break up beef in a kettle; add onion, garlic, green pepper and celery. Cook, stirring until beef is brown and vegetables are cooked. Add remaining ingredients EXCEPT beans. Cook over moderate heat about 30 minutes. Add beans and cook 15 minutes longer. (Serves 8)

Sam's Chili

Mrs. Sam Mosholder -- Bellevue, Washington

1 lb. GROUND BEEF
1 ONION
1 can (16-oz.) KIDNEY BEANS
1 can (16-oz.) REFRIED BEANS
1 can (8-oz.) TOMATO SAUCE
1 can (8-oz.) WATER
4 Tbsp. CELERY
1/8 cup GREEN PEPPER
¼ tsp. hot RED PEPPER
SALT and PEPPER to taste
1 tsp. PAPRIKA
1/8 tsp. GARLIC SALT
2 tsp. mild CHILI POWDER
¼ tsp. WORCESTERSHIRE
1 drop prepared MUSTARD
½ tsp. MOLASSES
½ tsp. BROWN SUGAR

Brown the beef with the onion and drain. Chop the celery, green pepper and hot red pepper very fine. Combine all ingredients and simmer at least two hours. (Serves 4)

Prospector's Chili

Nellie Howard -- Yuma, Arizona

1 lb. PINK BEANS
3 quarts WATER
1 brick CHILI
1 Tbsp. Cooking OIL
1 lb. GROUND BEEF
1 ONION (chopped)
½ clove GARLIC
1 tsp. CHILI POWDER
1 tsp. FLOUR
½ tsp. BLACK PEPPER
1 can (15-0z.) Del Monte
   TOMATO SAUCE
1 can WATER

Wash beans and put them into three quarts water in a large pot. Add brick chili and cook over medium heat. Heat oil in a skillet, and add meat, onions, and garlic. Stir frequently until beef loses red color. Then add chili powder, flour, black pepper and stir. Gradually add tomato sauce and water and cook over medium heat 10 minutes, stirring often. Add meat mixture to cooking beans and cook 1 to 2 hours on low. (Serves 8)

Pronto   Chili

Loraine Soik -- San Jose, California

3 Tbsp. OIL
1 lb. GROUND BEEF
1 1/3 cups ONION (chopped fine)
2½ cups canned KIDNEY BEANS
   (Dark red)
1 can (15-oz.) TOMATO SAUCE
1 tsp. SALT
1 Tbsp. FLOUR
2½ Tbsp. CHILI POWDER
3 Tbsp. WATER

Heat oil in large frying pan. Cook meat in pan until slightly browned. Add onions, stirring often with wooden spoon, and cook til onions are soft. To meat mixture, add beans (undrained) and tomato sauce. Cook for 15 minutes on medium heat, stirring often.

In small mixing bowl, combine salt, flour, chili powder and water. Add to meat, cover pan and simmer 50 minutes. Stir occasionally. (Serves 6 to 8)

Quick Chili

Mrs. D. E. Lukens -- Santa Cruz, California

½ lb. ground SUET
1 lb. HAMBURGER
1 tsp. MSG
2 BOUILLON CUBES
3 Tbsp. CHILI POWDER
1 Tbsp. CUMIN
1 tsp. crushed CORIANDER
SALT to taste
1 lg. ONION (chopped)
6 cloves GARLIC
1 can (4-oz.) chopped GREEN
  CHILES
1 pint canned TOMATOES
1 pint PINTO BEANS (cooked)

Brown hamburger and suet. Pour off grease. Add all seasonings and stir. Add onion, garlic, chiles and tomatoes. Simmer 20 minutes. Add cooked beans and simmer 10 minutes. (Serves 2)

Chili con Carne con Frijoles

Courtesy Heublein -- Grocery Products Group

2 lbs. Ground BEEF
1 cup ONION (chopped)
¾ cup GREEN PEPPER (chopped)
2 med. cloves GARLIC (minced)
1 can (28-oz.) WHOLE TOMATOES
  (chopped)
3 tsp. SALT
1 BAY LEAF
1 Tbsp. CHILI POWDER
2 cans (4-oz.) Ortega Diced
  GREEN CHILES
1 can (16-oz.) PINTO BEANS (drained)

In a 10-inch skillet, brown beef until crumbled. Drain. Add onion, green pepper, and garlic. Cook until vegetables are soft.

Stir in remaining ingredients EXCEPT beans. Simmer, covered, for 35 minutes, stirring occasionally. Remove cover. Mix in beans. Simmer, uncovered, 10 minutes, or until desired consistency. Garnish with sour cream or Jack cheese. (Serves 6 to 8)

Pat's Special Diet Chili

Pat Plumleigh -- Stanton, California

3 lbs. GROUND MEAT
1 Red ONION (chopped)
2 BELL PEPPERS (chopped)
1 can (46-oz.) TOMATO JUICE
2 cans French Cut GREEN BEANS
¾ jar (3½-oz.) CHILI POWDER
1 tsp. CUMIN
GARLIC POWDER to taste
SALT and PEPPER
2 packets Artificial Sweetener

Brown meat and drain fat. Combine meat with other ingredients into large pot and cook to chili consistency. (Serves 6)

Grandpa's Chile con Carne

Courtesy Hayden Flour Mills -- Tempe, Arizona

2 lbs. GROUND BEEF
SALT and PEPPER
GARLIC SALT
1 cup CELERY (with leaves)
MARGARINE
3 cans (#303) TOMATOES
2 cans (6-oz.) TOMATO PASTE
2 Tbsp. SUGAR
1 Tbsp. SALT
1/3 Tbsp. PEPPER
1 lb. Rose Brand PINTO BEANS (cooked)
1 can OLIVES (pitted and quartered)
Dash of OREGANO
½ cup PARSLEY
1 Tbsp. Worcestershire Sauce
2 to 4 Tbsp. CHILI POWDER
CAYENNE PEPPER
TABASCO Sauce
BAY LEAF
½ cup ONION (chopped)

Coat beef with salt and pepper and garlic salt. Saute beef and celery in margarine. Cover and simmer 10 minutes. Stir occasionally. Add tomatoes and tomato paste, sugar, salt, pepper, beans, olives, oregano, parsley and Worcestershire. Simmer 5 to 10 minutes. Taste and add remaining seasonings. (Serves 6 to 8)

Cowboy Chili Beans

Vincent L. Deibert -- San Jose, California

2 lbs. Red or Pink BEANS
1 Tbsp. BAKING SODA
3 Tbsp. BACON FAT
1 lg. ONION
1 fresh GREEN PEPPER
1 lg. fresh TOMATO
1 lb. GROUND BEEF
1 can (15-oz.) TOMATO SAUCE with mushrooms
2 BAY LEAVES
1 Tbsp. OREGANO
CHILI POWDER to taste
SALT to taste
¼ lb. SALT PORK (¾" cubes)
1 can BEER

Soak beans overnight with water and soda to cover. In morning, drain and wash beans well. Put beans into 5-quart, heavy gauge pot, with water to cover about 3'' over beans. Cook about three hours (or until tender).

Heat bacon grease in a skillet, and add onion, pepper and tomato. Brown for about 15 minutes. Add ground beef and simmer 1/2 hour. Add tomato sauce and simmer 1/2 hour more. Add meat mixture to cooked beans and stir. Add bay leaves, oregano, chili powder, salt, salt pork cubes and beer. Simmer for two hours. (Serves 6)

Betty's Favorite Chili

Betty Rogers -- El Monte, California

2 lbs. GROUND ROUND
1 small ONION (minced)
3 rounded Tbsp. CHILI POWDER
2 cans (27-oz.) small Red
   KIDNEY BEANS
5 cups TOMATO JUICE
¼ cup BROWN SUGAR (packed)
1 teaspoon SALT
1 teaspoon PEPPER

Brown meat and onion in large skillet. Add chili powder and simmer five minutes. Add beans, tomato juice, sugar, salt and pepper. Cover and simmer two hours. (Serves 6 to 8)

Paulsell's Elk Meat Champ Chili

Robert M. Paulsell -- Phoenix, Arizona

1 lb. PINTO BEANS
2 lbs. RUMP ROAST of ELK
1 can (15-oz.) Contadina TOMATO PUREE
2 med. ONIONS (chopped)
1 Tbsp. fresh CUMIN
5 Tbsp. fresh CHILI POWDER
SALT to taste

Presoak beans overnight. Cook beans in a slow cooker or a big pot.

Add meat to beans when they are well soaked. Add puree and onions. (Onions should be chopped extra fine.)

Stir in chili powder, cumin and salt. Cook until meat is done and beans are tender. Cooking time is about four hours on top of the stove. (Serves 6 to 10)

Pete's Chili

Peter Vann -- Saratoga, California

1 to 2 Tbsp. BUTTER
1 lg. ONION (sliced)
1 GREEN PEPPER (chopped)
1½ lbs. GROUND BEEF
3 cups canned KIDNEY BEANS
1 can (28-oz.) TOMATOES
1 can (15-oz.) TOMATO SAUCE
2 Tbsp. CHILI POWDER
3 tsp. SALT
1 BAY LEAF

Brown onion, green pepper and meat in fat. Add all ingredients, cover, and simmer about an hour. (Grandma's Spanish Seasoning may substitute for chili powder.)(Serves 6)

Chile-Chili Societies

International Chili Society
P.O. Box 2966
Newport Beach, CA 92663

Chili Appreciation Society
International
P.O. Box 31183
Dallas, Texas 75231

International Connoisseurs
of Green & Red Chile
P.O. Box 3467
Las Cruces, N. M. 88003

A handful of chile lovers and their devotion to the chile mystique has blossomed into a world-wide society -- the International Connoisseurs of Green and Red Chile. Originally designed to socially draw together lovers of the pod, the organization now is multi-purposeful.

Recipes with Chiles

To begin with, it encourages chile research through grants, spreads the chile culture via cooking classes and demonstrations on educational television, publishes cookbooks, distributes seeds with instructions for growing, and provides chile survival kits to those chile lovers who suffer withdrawal pains in areas where chile is not accessible.

In addition, this non-profit organization, with headquarters at New Mexico State University, now boasts sub-chapters throughout the United States and the world. Its members gather regularly to dine on chile dishes and to concoct new chile recipes.

They have succeeded in enlightening the public to the fact that green and red chile represent different stages in the ripening of the fruit. Chile pods emerge with green coloring. Left on the vine, they will turn red, and are often entwined into decorative festoons and hung to dry.

Chile peppers may be chopped, crushed, canned, dried, frozen, pickled -- or, as hardy souls will attest -- eaten raw. Some of the more common varieties include: the Anaheim green or red (commonly called the California chile), a long, slender, mild pepper; the Pasilla (also dubbed the Ancho), similar to the Anaheim, but with a slightly bitter taste; the Yellow Wax (frequently acclaimed as "yellow hots") with waxy, shiny texture; the Hungarian Yellow Wax (a tapering pepper, ideal for sauces or pickling); the New Mexico No.6-4 (a thick-fleshed, early maturing pepper); the Rio Grande 21 (a large, medium pungent pepper popular with commercial processors); the Jalapeno (a short, stubby, very dark green pepper) ideal for adding "hotness" to sauces; the Serrano (possibly one of the hottest chiles available), dark green, but shorter and thinner than the Jalapeno; the Sandia A (a sizzling native New Mexico pepper), and the Nu-Mex Big Jim (a fleshy pod with medium pungency).

Concentrated chile research began in 1907, when Dr. Fabian Garcia (horticulturist and later director of NMSU Agricultural Extension Service) determined to improve native chile through plant breeding. More recent developments have been credited to Dr. Roy Nakayama (considered the world's foremost chile expert) and his staff at NMSU.

Fresh Red Chile Sauce

14 to 24 fresh RED CHILES (or 1 cup frozen chiles)
1 tsp. SALT
1 clove GARLIC
1 small ONION (sliced)
1 tsp. OREGANO
½ cup WATER
1 Tbsp. BUTTER (or margarine)

Remove stems, seeds, and veins of fresh red chile. Cover with boiling water and let stand 10 minutes. Remove chile and place with salt, garlic, onion, and oregano in blender. Add water, according to blender requirements, and blend until all ingredients are reduced to a smooth paste.

Put sauce into heavy pan. Add 1/2 cup water (or more, depending on the amount used in blending). Add butter or margarine. Simmer about 1/2 hour, or until mixture has the desired consistency. Stir occasionally to keep from burning. (Makes about 1 1/2 cups)

Fresh Salsa de Chile Verde

Rosita Keene -- owner of Rosita's Mexican & American Restaurant, Tempe, Arizona

6 Fresh GREEN CHILES
2 YELLOW HOT CHILES
2 JALAPENOS (pickled)
¼ cup JALAPENO JUICE
6 Fresh TOMATOES
¼ cup White VINEGAR
3 tsp. SALT
1 tsp. PEPPER
1 tsp. Mexican OREGANO
6 sprigs Fresh Green CILANTRO
1 fresh clove GARLIC (diced or pureed)

Green chiles and yellow hots should be roasted, peeled and diced. (Canned chiles may be substituted.) Tomatoes should be roasted in a deep fryer, then steamed in a wet towel, peeled and diced. Combine all ingredients and let sit--the longer the better. Use as topping for tacos, burros, eggs, and other dishes.

Dry Red Chile Sauce

Whole pods may be used to make red chile sauce. Since the pungency is largely in the veins of the chile, remove the veins for a milder sauce.

Strainer Method

Remove stem, seeds, and veins from 14 to 24 chile pods. Wash pods in warm water. Place pods in a pan and cover with hot water. Heat to almost a boil. Remove the pan from heat and let the pods stand in the water for one hour (or until the pulp separates easily from the tough outer skin. Put through a ricer o colander, adding enough water to remove the pulp. If sauce is very thick, thin with water to desired consistency. Add salt to taste.

Blender Method

Remove stems, seeds, and veins from 14 to 24 chile pods. Wash and drain. Spread on cookie sheet and dry chile in a warm oven (200 to 250 F), turning frequently. Leave oven door open. Chile burns easily, giving the sauce an undesirable flavor. Remove chile to pan, cover with hot water, let boil for 10 minutes (or until pulp is soft and separates from skin.). Use the cooking water for the required amount of liquid. Blend until a smooth paste is acquired. Strain, if desired. Add salt to taste.

Red Chile Sauce

24 dried RED CHILES
2 Tbsp. FAT
2 cloves GARLIC (chopped)
2 ONIONS (sliced)
2 Tbsp. FLOUR
1 tsp. SALT
½ tsp. OREGANO
1 cup TOMATO JUICE

Wash chiles, remove stems and seeds. Cover with water and boil for 30 minutes. Sieve or put through a food mill. Heat fat and saute onions and garlic. Add flour and stir to make a smooth paste. Combine flour mixture with red chili pulp. Add salt, oregano and tomato juice; simmer 1/2 hour.

Chili Paste Salsa

Courtesy Gene and Judy England -- Santa Cruz Chili & Spice Co.
Amado and Tumacacori, Arizona

1 clove GARLIC
2 Tbsp. OIL
2 Tbsp. FLOUR
1 to 2 Tbsp. Santa Cruz CHILI PASTE
1 cup WATER (or beef broth)

Pound garlic, brown in oil and remove. Stir in flour and
brown. Add chili paste mixed with water or beef broth. Cook
and stir until thick. Add other seasonings as desired. The
salsa is good over enchiladas, hamburgers, or baked chicken.

Beef Broth

Cube and brown 1/2 pound beef chuck. Add water to cover
and simmer, covered, until tender. This broth may be used
in place of water in the Chili Paste Salsa recipe.

Marti's Salsa

Marti Combel -- Phoenix, Arizona

1 can (16-oz.) STEWED TOMATOES
1 can (7-oz.) diced GREEN CHILES
1 sm. bunch GREEN ONIONS
1 CHILE TEPIN (crushed)
Dash GARLIC SALT
SALT and PEPPER to taste

Pour tomatoes and diced chili into a large bowl. Chop tops
of green onions and add to bowl. Add garlic salt and salt
and pepper to taste. Squash the mixture together by hand.
Crush one chiletepin and add to mixture. Stir and serve.

Taco Sauce

Courtesy Santa Maria Chili, Inc. -- Santa Maria, Calif.

8 to 12 lg. GREEN CHILES
1 med. ripe TOMATO
½ tsp. SALT

Remove stems, seeds and veins from chiles. Peel tomato
and finely mince chiles. Mash tomato until almost liquid, and
add to chiles, together with salt. (Sauce will keep, covered,
in refrigerator up to five days.)

Sombrero Chili Dip

Courtesy Heublein -- Grocery Products Group

1 lb. ground BEEF
¼ cup ONION (minced)
1 med. clove GARLIC (minced)
1 can (8-oz.) TOMATO SAUCE
1 can (7-oz.) Ortega Diced
  GREEN CHILES
1 can (16-oz.) KIDNEY BEANS
  (drained and mashed)
1 tsp. SALT

Garnish
½ cup (1/8 lb.) LONGHORN
  CHEESE (grated)
¼ cup RIPE OLIVES (sliced)
¼ cup ONION (chopped)

In a 10-inch skillet, brown beef until crumbled. Drain. Add onion and garlic. Cook until onion is soft. Mix in tomato sauce, chiles, beans and salt. Heat thoroughly. Place in chafing dish, topped with garnishes. Serve hot with corn chips for dipping. (Serves 6 to 8)

Chili Sauce

Courtesy Santa Maria Chili, Inc. -- Santa Maria, Calif.

1 lb. CHILI PODS
2 quarts WATER
1 clove GARLIC
1 tsp. SALT
1 tsp. OREGANO

Wash, clean and remove stems and seeds from chili pods. Soak chili pods in lukewarm water until soft. Add garlic, salt and oregano. Beat with electric mixer (or blender) until smooth and creamy. (Makes about two quarts.)

Chilaquiles

FAT (for frying)
1 doz. TORTILLAS
2 cups CHILI SAUCE
1 clove GARLIC - mashed
1 small ONION (chopped fine)
1 cup CHEESE (grated)
SALT (to taste)

Cut tortillas into bite-size pieces. Heat fat and fry tortilla pieces until toasted and crisp. Drain on paper towels. Heat chili sauce and add drained tortilla pieces. Stir in garlic and onions. Allow to simmer until tortillas are almost dry. Transfer to hot platter and top with cheese.

Chile con Queso Dip #1

Courtesy Santa Maria Chili, Inc. -- Santa Maria, Calif.

1 clove GARLIC (minced)
1 med. ONION (minced fine)
2 Tbsp. FAT
1 cup GREEN CHILI SAUCE
½ cup EVAPORATED MILK
½ lb. Process CHEESE (cubed)

Combine garlic, onion and fat in top portion of a double boiler. Cook at medium heat until onion is transparent. Add green chili sauce and bring to a boil. Remove from heat and add milk and cheese. Place over boiling water and cook, stirring often until cheese melts. Lower heat and simmer 1/2 hour. Cool to room temperature to serve as spread or dip.

Chile con Queso Dip #2

2 Tbsp. BUTTER
½ cup ONION (chopped)
1 can (4-oz.) GREEN CHILES (chopped)
1 cup Whole TOMATOES (drained)
SALT and PEPPER to taste
½ lb. JACK CHEESE
¾ cup LIGHT CREAM

Cook and stir onion in butter over medium heat for about five minutes. Stir in chiles, tomatoes, salt and pepper. Simmer 15 minutes. When cheese begins to melt, stir in cream. Cook and stir until cheese is melted; cook 10 minutes longer. Serve in chafing dish to keep hot.

Salsa Supreme

1 can (14-oz.) TOMATOES
1 can (4-oz.) GREEN CHILES
1 med. ONION
2 Tbsp. OIL
2 Tbsp. VINEGAR
   SALT to taste

Combine tomatoes, chiles and onion and put through a grinder. Add oil and vinegar. Season with salt to taste.

Sterling's Salsa

Sterling Hebbard -- Phoenix, Arizona

2 cups canned TOMATOES
1 can (4-oz.) CHILES
2 med. ONIONS
2 cloves GARLIC
1 Tbsp. CHILI POWDER
½ tsp. SALT
Coarse BLACK PEPPER
1 Tbsp. White VINEGAR

Cut tomatoes into small pieces in a mixing bowl. Remove seeds and white core from chiles and dice. Add to tomatoes, together with diced onions and crushed garlic cloves. Add remaining ingredients and mix thoroughly. Taste for salt. Cover and refrigerate at least three hours before using. (Salsa will last two weeks in refrigerator; several months in freezer.)

Green Chile Sauce

4 lg. GREEN TOMATOES
4 GREEN CHILES
1 Tbsp. ONION (minced)
1 Tbsp. PARSLEY (minced)
SALT and PEPPER
½ cup OIL

Cover tomatoes, chiles, onion and parsley in water and cook until vegetables are soft. Press through a strainer, add salt and pepper. Heat oil and add chili mixture to it; cook 15 minutes.

Green Chile Relish

1 lb. GREEN CHILES
¼ cup VINEGAR
½ tsp. SALT
¼ cup WATER
2 Tbsp. OLIVE OIL

Wash chiles. Remove stems and seeds. Grind through a food chopper. Mix all ingredients in saucepan and cook slowly for 20 minutes, stirring occasionally. Serve as cold relish.

Guacamole

4 AVOCADOS
2 med. TOMATOES
4 YELLOW HOT CHILES
1 clove GARLIC (minced)
1 small ONION (minced)
1 tsp. SALT
1 tsp. LEMON JUICE

Cut avocados in half; remove pit. Peel skin and mash pulp with a fork until creamy. Roast and peel tomatoes and chiles. Combine tomatoes, chiles, and garlic in blender and blend well. Combine with mashed avocados and remaining ingredients.

Chili Butter

Courtesy Gebhardt's Mexican Foods -- San Antonio, Texas

4 Tbsp. BUTTER
½ tsp. SALT
1 tsp. Gebhardt's CHILI POWDER
½ clove GARLIC (minced)
2 Tbsp. LEMON JUICE

Cream butter; add all ingredients and blend well. Spread on roasting or broiling meat.

Barbecue Sauce

Courtesy Gebhardt's Mexican Foods -- San Antonio, Texas

½ cup BUTTER
1 small ONION (minced)
1 clove GARLIC (minced)
1½ tsp. DRY MUSTARD
2 Tbsp. Gebhardt's CHILI POWDER
1 cup TOMATO CATSUP
½ cup VINEGAR
½ cup WATER
1 Tbsp. SUGAR
1 Tbsp. Worcestershire Sauce

Saute onion and garlic in butter. Add other ingredients and boil five minutes (or until thick). Use sauce for broiling or roasting meat.

Sopa de Albondigas (Meatball Soup)

Soup

8 cups WATER
2 tsp. SALT
1 Tbsp. FAT
¼ cup ONION (chopped)
¼ cup GREEN CHILE (diced)
½ BELL PEPPER (diced)
1 clove GARLIC (minced)
½ cup fresh TOMATOES (diced)

Add salt to water in a large pot, and bring to a boil. Heat fat in skillet, add onion, chiles, pepper, and garlic and saute until golden. Add sauteed vegetables to boiling water, together with fresh tomatoes. Lower heat to simmer.

Meatballs

1 lb. GROUND BEEF
¼ cup raw RICE
1 EGG
2 cloves GARLIC (minced)
2 tsp. SALT
½ tsp. BLACK PEPPER
¼ tsp. CUMIN
1 Tbsp. chopped MINT LEAVES

Combine all ingredients in large mixing bowl. Form into tightly packed meatballs and drop into simmering liquid. Simmer for 45 to 50 minutes. (Serves 8 to 10)

Chile Cheese Soup

1 Tbsp. cooking OIL
1 ONION (chopped)
1 can (7-oz.) GREEN CHILE (diced)
1 can (7-oz.) TOMATO SAUCE
6 to 7 cups WATER
SALT
1 POTATO (diced)
2 cloves GARLIC (minced)
½ lb. LONGHORN (grated)

Use cooking oil to lightly fry onion. When frying is completed, add chiles and tomatoes and cook for 10 minutes. Add water, salt, potatoes and garlic. Simmer until potatoes are done. Add cheese, stir and serve. (Serves 6 to 8)

Caldo Ultimo! (The Last Word in Soup)

Meridee Wynn -- Santa Fe, N. M. (Courtesy ICGRC)

1 lb. lean GROUND BEEF (coarse ground)
1 lg. ONION (chopped)
1 clove GARLIC (minced)
WATER to cover
1 lg. POTATO (diced)
2 APPLES (sliced thin)
½ cup Whole ALMONDS (raw or blanched)
2 cups TOMATO JUICE
¼ tsp. crushed CUMIN SEEDS
¼ tsp. crushed OREGANO LEAVES
4 cans (4-oz.) GREEN CHILES (chopped)
½ cup RAISINS
Juice of 1 LIME
SALT and PEPPER to taste

In a heavy Dutch oven, brown meat well, stirring frequently. Add onion and garlic and cook over medium heat until onion is limp. Add water to cover and simmer covered for 1/2 hour (or until meat is tender), adding more water, if needed, to keep meat covered.

Add potato, apples, almonds, tomato juice, cumin, oregano, and two cans green chiles. Simmer until potato is tender. Add lime juice and raisins and cook over low heat for five minutes. Add salt and pepper. (Soup tastes best if cooled with the lid off, and then placed covered in refrigerator for 24 hours.) Remove any accumulated fat from top, re-heat, and serve. Put remaining two cans chiles into bowl to be passed at table and stirred into soup. (Serves 4 to 6)

Chile Beans

½ lb. RED or PINTO BEANS
4 cups WATER
1 tsp. SALT
1 tsp. CHILI POWDER
¼ tsp. crushed RED PEPPER
½ cup ONION (chopped fine)

Sort and wash beans. Add water, bring to a boil, cover tightly and cook 2 minutes. Remove from heat (covered), and let soak one hour. Add remaining ingredients. Bring to a boil, cover tightly, continue cooking slowly, stirring occasionally, for 1 1/2 to 2 hours (until beans are tender). Add more water, if needed, to keep beans from sticking. (Makes about 3 cups)

Western Baked Beans

3 cups PINTO BEANS
1 clove GARLIC (minced)
1 tsp. SALT
2 small ONIONS
½ cup BROWN SUGAR
1 tsp. CHILE POWDER
¾ cup canned TOMATO
3 slices BACON

Cover beans with water and soak overnight. Heat to boiling point the water in which the beans were soaked. Add beans, garlic and salt, and simmer one hour. Drain the beans, saving the liquid. Put beans and whole onions into casserole. Sprinkle beans with sugar (or sorghum molasses) and chile powder. Cover beans with strained tomato and one cup of reserved bean liquid. Arrange bacon (or 1/2 cup diced salt pork) on top. Cover and bake in 300 oven for five hours. Add more bean liquid, if necessary. (Serves 8 to 10)

Eggplant & Green Chile

1 lg. EGGPLANT
1 EGG
2 cups SOFT BREAD CRUMBS
6 strips BACON
1 small ONION (diced)
1 cup GREEN CHILE (chopped)
SALT and PEPPER to taste

Peel eggplant. Cut into cubes and cook in salted water until tender. Cool slightly after draining well. Mash eggplant. Combine onions, well-beaten egg, chile, bread crumbs, salt and pepper. Add to eggplant and mix well. Put in buttered casserole, top with bacon strips and bake in 350 F oven for 45 minutes. (Serves 4)

Chili Rice

Omie (Mrs. Henry) Marchbanks -- Levelland, Texas

1 cup RICE
¼ cup BUTTER
2 tsp. SALT
2 tsp. CHILI POWDER

Brown rice in butter (or margarine). Add salt and chile powder. Pour enough boiling water to cover one inch above rice. Cover and simmer for 30 minutes. Sprinkle with grated cheese or top with one tablespoon of chili. (Serves 4)

Green Chile and Squash

7 to 12 GREEN CHILES
1 Tbsp. FAT
2 cups SUMMER SQUASH (cubed)
1 small ONION (chopped)
SALT to taste
1 cup Fresh or Frozen CORN (optional)

Prepare chile. Saute chopped onion slightly. Add squash and corn. Cook slowly in little or no water until tender. Add chopped chile and salt and serve. (Serves 6 to 8)

Mexican Corn

1 Tbsp. OLIVE OIL (or cooking oil)
1 ONION (chopped fine)
2 cups TOMATO PUREE
2 Tbsp. CHILE POWDER
2 Tbsp. BUTTER
SALT and PEPPER to taste
3 cups uncooked CORN (cut from cob)

Saute onion in hot oil until golden yellow. In a large mixing bowl, combine remaining ingredients. Add sauteed onions and mix well. Pour into buttered casserole and bake in a 350 F oven for one hour. (Serves 6)

Chile Succotash

1 pkg. Frozen LIMA BEANS
1 pkg. Frozen CORN
4 GREEN CHILES (chopped)
2 Tbsp. ONION (chopped)
2 EGGS (beaten)
2 Tbsp. CATSUP
¼ cup WATER
1 tsp. SALT
3 Tbsp. soft MARGARINE

In a casserole dish, place lima beans, corn (cooked and drained), chiles and onion. Mix remaining ingredients together and pour over vegetables. Stir slightly and bake in a 325 F oven for 45 minutes. (Serves 4)

Frijoles Borrachos (Drunken Beans)

1 lb. PINTO BEANS
1 med. ONION (diced)
5 to 6 cups WATER
3 fresh TOMATOES
4 GREEN CHILES (diced)
2 cloves GARLIC (diced)
1 can BEER
SALT to taste

Wash and sort pinto beans. Add onion and water to beans and bring to boiling point. Remove from heat and cover for two hours. Peel tomatoes, and chop into small chunks. Add tomatoes, chiles, garlic and beer to beans, bring to second boil. Reduce heat and simmer from five to six hours. Add salt half an hour before serving. (Serves 6 to 8)

Spinach with Chili Seeds & Garlic

Lola Armijo -- Tempe, Arizona

3 bunches fresh SPINACH
5 lg. GREEN ONIONS
2 Tbsp. BACON GREASE (or shortening)
½ tsp. GARLIC POWDER
1/8 cup CHILI SEEDS
1 cup plain unsalted cooked BEANS
1 tsp. SALT

Cook cleaned spinach in water to barely cover. The leaves should be torn apart and not cooked through.

Saute the chopped green onion (tops included). Cook until soft. To the green onion, add partially cooked spinach and 1/2 cup spinach liquid. Add remaining ingredients and cook 10 minutes more. (Serves 4 to 6)

Green Chile and Potatoes

4 fresh GREEN CHILES (chopped)
1 Tbsp. Cooking FAT
1 med. ONION (chopped)
1 clove GARLIC (chopped)
2 cups POTATOES (diced--raw or cooked)
SALT to taste
Boiling Water

Prepare chile. Slightly saute onion and garlic. Add chopped chile and diced potatoes. If cooked potatoes are used, add water to cover and boil 10 minutes. Cook raw potatoes until tender. (Serves 4)

Green Chile Casserole

Jacquelyn Berger -- Scottsdale, Arizona

4 whole CHICKEN BREASTS (boned)
6 to 8 CORN TORTILLAS
1 can CREAM of MUSHROOM SOUP
1 can CREAM of CHICKEN SOUP
½ cup MILK
1 ONION (chopped)
1 can (7-oz.) GREEN CHILE (chopped)
SALT and PEPPER
Grated CHEESE

Bone chicken and cut into pieces. Cut tortillas into one-inch strips. Mix soup, milk and onions.

Butter a 3 or 4-quart casserole and cover bottom with soup mixture. Add a layer of tortilla strips and chunks of chicken. Top with layer of chilis.

Add remainder of soup mix and top with grated cheese. Bake (covered) in a 300 F oven for one hour. (Serves 4)

Chili Meat Loaf

2 lbs. GROUND BEEF
1 lb. GROUND PORK
½ lb. GROUND HAM
1 cup CRACKER CRUMBS
2 EGGS
1 Tbsp. CHILI POWDER

½ cup MILK
2 Tbsp. ONION (minced)
1 tsp. SALT
½ clove GARLIC (minced)
6 drops TABASCO Sauce

Combine ingredients in large mixing bowl and mix thoroughly. Turn into meat loaf pan; pour water over top and bake in 350 F oven for 50 minutes. (Baste often.) (Serves 6)

Chili-Potato Casserole

W. Wirship -- Corona, California

1 Tbsp. SALAD OIL
1 lb. GROUND BEEF
1 med. ONION (chopped)

1 lg. POTATO (sliced thick)
1 pint CHILI (no beans)
1 can (#303) KIDNEY BEANS
3 small fresh TOMATOES

Pour salad oil into bottom of casserole. Layer beef, onions, potatoes, chili, beans and tomatoes; repeat layers in sequence indicated. Bake in a 350 F oven for 1 1/2 hours. (Serves 8)

Chimichangas (Stuffed Flour Tortillas)

12 FLOUR TORTILLAS
2¼ cups MEAT FILLING
OIL for frying

Spoon 3 tablespoons meat filling down center of tortilla. Fold ends and roll tortilla tightly around filling, fastening with toothpick. (Prepare only 3 or 4 at a time, because the tortilla will absorb liquid from filling.) Fry in hot oil, turning until golden (about 1 to 2 minutes). Remove from fat and drain on thick layers of paper towels. Keep in warm oven until all are cooked. Serve garnished with cheese, lettuce and green onions. (Serves 4)

Meat Filling

1 lb. GROUND BEEF
1 small ONION (chopped)
1 tsp. OREGANO
½ tsp. GARLIC POWDER
1/8 tsp. CUMIN
2 tsp. RED CHILE POWDER (or 3 Tbsp. GREEN CHILE, chopped)

Garnish

1½ cups GREEN ONIONS
1½ cups shredded LETTUCE
2 cups CHEDDAR (shredded)

Crumble ground beef in skillet, add onion and spices and simmer until meat is cooked. Add chile or chile powder and remove from heat while flavors blend.

Chile Verde

Iclia (Mrs. O. J.) Wilkinson -- Paradise Valley, Arizona

1 Tbsp. OLIVE OIL
1 ONION (chopped)
2 cloves GARLIC (chopped)
3 lbs. PORK SHOULDER
    (bite-size cubes)
1 can (28-oz.) TOMATOES
2 cans (4-oz.) GREEN CHILES
    (chopped)
1 cup WATER
SALT to taste

Saute onion and garlic in olive oil in a Dutch oven. Remove onion and garlic and brown meat in same pan. Return onion and garlic to meat, along with other ingredients. Cook slowly for one hour (or until meat is done). Best prepared a day in advance. To reheat, simmer one-half hour. (Serves 4)

Carne Enchilada

Lola Armijo -- Tempe, Arizona

(Carne enchilada is similar to barbecued meat, and in this case, does not refer to the familiar rolled corn tortilla dish.)

1 Boston Butt PORK ROAST
(3½ to 5 lbs.)
1 quart CHILI PASTE

(Other boneless roast can be substituted for pork) Cut roast into strips, approximately 1'' x 4''. Arrange meat in baking pan. Pour chili paste over meat. The meat should be well coated with extra sauce in bottom of pan. Bake in 450 F oven for one hour. Turn meat at 1/2 hour. There will be a lot of liquid at the halfway point. In the next 1/2 hour, the sauce will become thick and cling to the meat.

Chili Paste (Raw Chili)

12 pods New Mexico HOT DRIED
RED CHILIS
2 cloves GARLIC
1 tsp. SALT
¼ tsp. OREGANO
1 quart WATER

Break chilis open. Remove most of seeds, stems, and any dark spots. Soak cleaned chilis in water (at least 1/2 hour). Drain chilis. Place in a blender with a quart of fresh water and remaining ingredients. Blend at high speed for five minutes.

Green Chile Grits

6 cups BOILING WATER
1½ cups GRITS
2 tsp. SALT
1½ sticks BUTTER (melted)
1 lb. Mild CHEDDAR (grated)
3 EGGS (well-beaten)
½ can PIMENTO
1 can (4-oz.) GREEN CHILE
(chopped)

Boil water, grits and salt until thick. Combine remaining ingredients and add to grits. Pour into greased baking dish and bake (uncovered) in 300 F oven for one hour. (Serves 4)

Enchiladas

Cover hot fried tortilla with Mexican cheese sauce, then add chile sauce. Repeat this process until three tortillas are stacked. Cover with cheese and chile sauces. Sprinkle with grated cheese.

Place enchiladas in 325 F oven until cheese melts. Serve on piping hot plate. (Serves 3)

Fried Tortillas

9 TORTILLAS
FAT for frying
½ cup CHEESE (grated)

Heat fat below smoking point in skillet. Fry the tortillas. (Do not fry too crisp or they will break.) Drain on paper.

Mexican Cheese Sauce

2 Tbsp. BUTTER (or margarine)
2 Tbsp. GREEN CHILE (chopped)
1 tsp. SALT
1 tsp. CHILE POWDER
1 tsp. DRY MUSTARD
1 Tbsp. FLOUR
1 cup TOMATO JUICE
1 cup cooked CORN
1½ cups AMERICAN CHEESE (grated)
1 EGG

Melt butter in top of double boiler. Then saute the chopped pepper over direct heat. Add seasonings, flour, tomato juice, and corn. Stir constantly until smooth. Place over water and cook for five minutes. Add grated cheese. Allow it to melt slowly. Beat egg and add to the hot mixture.

Enchilada Sauce

2 Tbsp. BUTTER (or margarine)
½ cup ONIONS (chopped fine)
2 Tbsp. FLOUR
2 Tbsp. CHILE POWDER
1 tsp. SALT
WATER

Melt butter in a saucepan and fry onions lightly until golden. Add flour and blend well. Add chile powder, salt, and water and cook until thick, stirring constantly.

Green Corn Tamales

Jewell (Mrs. Delbert) Lewis -- Coolidge, Arizona

> 36 ears GREEN CORN (unhusked Mexican June corn)
> 4 lbs. LONGHORN CHEESE (grated)
> 1 can Ortega's GREEN CHILI STRIPS
> ½ cup SALT (or to taste)
> 1½ lbs. MARGARINE (or lard)
> Small curd Cottage Cheese (optional)

Begin with unhusked corn. To get husks without tearing them, cut off about one inch from the stem end of the ear. Roll the husks off carefully, wiping to clean. Throw away torn or narrow husks and save large husks for wrapping the tamales.

With a sharp knife, cut corn off the cob into a large container. Scrape the cob to get all the kernels out. Set aside some cobs. Put kernels through a corn grinder or heavy duty blender.

Mix softened margarine, salt and half the Longhorn cheese into the ground corn. This mixture is "masa." (If corn is dry, blend in enough cottage cheese to moisten. For moist, tender tamales, it is necessary to add a lot of cottage cheese.)

Cut green chili strips into 1/4 inch pieces and toss with remaining grated Longhorn cheese in a separate bowl.

To put masa on corn husks, follow these steps: spread about three tablespoons masa on one corner of a husk. Place one tablespoon chili-cheese mixture in middle of masa. Roll up in husk rather tightly and fold up pointed end. (If stuffing procedure takes a long time, keep the husks in warm water, then drain and pat dry before using.)

Line the bottom of a roaster with corncobs. Add water to cover the cobs (not the tamales). Place wrapped tamales with open end up in the roaster and steam about 45 minutes (or until tamales lose milky color). To freeze, wrap tamales in foil. Steam to use. (Makes about 6 dozen)

Huevos Rancheros

EGGS -- Ranch Style

2 medium ONIONS
3 fresh TOMATOES
2 GREEN CHILE PEPPERS

Minced PARSLEY
1 Tbsp. BUTTER
¼ tsp. SALT
6 EGGS

Chop onions, tomatoes and chile peppers. Brown with parsley in butter, add salt, and cook for five minutes. Fry eggs in separate pan and pour sauce over them. (Serves 2)

New Mexico Enchiladas

Pat (Mrs. Dan) Blatnik -- Phoenix, Arizona

1 quart RED CHILI SAUCE
SALT to taste
1 cup TOMATO JUICE
FLOUR for thickening
1 doz. CORN TORTILLAS
1 pkg. (12-oz.) CHEDDAR
  CHEESE (grated)
½ small ONION (diced)

Heat sauce. Add salt and tomato juice. Thicken slightly with flour or corn starch. Soak two or more tortillas at a time in the heated sauce until softened. Layer tortillas, cheese and onion in a stack (three per person). Top each with fried egg. Serve hot with extra sauce. (Serves 4)

Red Chili Sauce

30 Red CHILI PODS (dried)

Remove stems and seeds from pods. Wash pods well. Cover with water and boil about 10 to 15 minutes. Let pods cool for easier handling. Place peppers and liquid in blender. Blend to puree. Then pour through strainer to remove pepper skins. (Liquid may be stored in containers and frozen for future use.) (Makes between 3 and 4 quarts chili sauce.)

Sour Cream Green Enchiladas

Martha De Haven -- Los Alamos, N. M. (Courtesy ICGRC)

2/3 cup Cooking OIL
12 CORN TORTILLAS
½ lb. PROCESS CHEESE
1 can (4-oz.) GREEN CHILES (chopped)
½ ONION (chopped)
2 very ripe TOMATOES (chopped)
1 Tbsp. JALAPENO RELISH (or to taste)
1 tsp. SUGAR
1 cup SOUR CREAM
1 cup CHEDDAR (grated)

Fry tortillas in oil until tender and set aside. In a double boiler, combine cheese, chiles, onion, tomatoes, relish, and sugar. Heat and stir until cheese is melted. Blend in sour cream and reheat. Dip tortillas in sauce and stack (3 tortillas per serving) on heated plates, with grated cheese between and on top of tortillas. Heat in hot oven until cheese is melted. Garnish with shredded lettuce. (Serves 4)

Green Chile Burros

1½ lbs. BEEF ROUND
1 Tbsp. FAT
2 Tbsp. FLOUR
1 cup WATER
1/3 cup CHILE SAUCE
4 lg. FLOUR TORTILLAS

Meat should be ground or chopped fine. Heat fat, add meat, and cook slowly. Add salt to taste. When meat is done, add flour and brown. Add chile sauce, then water, and simmer until thickened. Spread 1/4 of mixture on each tortilla and roll up. (Serves 4)

Chili Sauce for Burros

1 med. TOMATO
2 GREEN CHILES
2 tsp. FLOUR
2 Tbsp. FAT

Toast tomato and chile and peel both. Remove seeds from chile. Mash until very smooth. Heat fat, add flour, add mashed tomato and chile. Cook, stirring constantly, until thickened.

Barbecued Chicken in Foil

Courtesy Gebhardt's Mexican Foods -- San Antonio, Texas

1½ to 2 lb. FRYING CHICKEN (disjointed)
3 Tbsp. KETCHUP
2 Tbsp. VINEGAR
1 Tbsp. LEMON JUICE
2 Tbsp. Worcestershire Sauce
¼ cup WATER
2 Tbsp. melted BUTTER
2 tsp. SALT
1 tsp. DRY MUSTARD
2 tsp. Gebhardt's CHILI POWDER
1 tsp. PAPRIKA
¼ tsp. RED PEPPER

Dip the pieces of cut-up chicken in the sauce made by combining the rest of the ingredients, and arrange in a single layer in aluminum foil. Spoon the sauce over the top.
Seal the foil tightly and place on a rack in a roaster. Bake in a 500 F oven for 15 minutes. Reduce heat to 350 F and continue to bake for 1 1/4 to 1 1/2 hours, or until the chicken is tender.

Chalupa (Roast Pork)

Jewell (Mrs. Delbert) Lewis -- Coolidge, Arizona

3 lb. PORK ROAST
1 lb. PINTO BEANS
2 cloves GARLIC (chopped)
2 Tbsp. CHILI POWDER
1 Tbsp. ground CUMIN
1 tsp. OREGANO
1 can GREEN CHILES (chopped)
1 Tbsp. SALT

Trim fat off roast, wash the beans, and combine all ingredients in a large pot. Cover with water. Cook, covered, over low heat, adding water as needed. After six hours cooking time, remove bones and break up roast. Continue to cook, uncovered, until thickened. Serve, burro style, on a large, warm flour tortilla. Or, serve on tostada shells, topped with chopped lettuce, tomatoes, avocado, onion, shredded cheese.

Mexican Spoon Bread

1 can (16-oz.) Cream-Style CORN
1 cup CORN MEAL
1/3 cup melted SHORTENING
2 EGGS (slightly beaten)
1 tsp. SALT
½ tsp. BAKING SODA
1 can (4-oz.) GREEN CHILIS (diced)
1½ cups CHEDDAR (shredded)

Combine first six ingredients and mix well. Pour half the batter into a greased 9x9x2" pan. Sprinkle with chiles and half the cheese. Pour on remaining batter. Sprinkle with remaining cheese. Bake in a 400 F oven for 45 minutes. Cool 10 minutes before cutting and serving with sauce. (Serves 8)

Spoon Bread Sauce

1 can (28-oz.) TOMATOES
1 can (8-oz.) TOMATO SAUCE
¼ cup GREEN CHILES (chopped)
1 tsp. SALT
Dash PEPPER
½ tsp. OREGANO
½ tsp. Cooking OIL

Combine all ingredients and mix well. Heat thoroughly.

Chili Pot Roast

4 to 5 lb. POT-ROAST
2 Tbsp. FLOUR
1 tsp. CHILI POWDER
1 Tbsp. PAPRIKA
2 tsp. SALT
3 Tbsp. LARD (or drippings)
2 med. ONIONS
16 whole CLOVES
1/3 cup WATER
1 stick CINNAMON
2 Tbsp. FLOUR
¼ cup WATER

Combine flour, chili powder, paprika and salt. Dredge pot-roast in seasoned flour. Brown pot-roast in lard or drippings. Pour off drippings. Stud each onion with 8 whole cloves. Add water, onions and cinnamon stick to meat. Cover and cook slowly for 2 1/2 to 3 hours (until tender). Remove meat to hot platter. Discard onions and cinnamon stick. Measure cooking liquid and add water to make 2 cups. Make a roux with flour and 1/4 cup water. Add to cooking liquid, stirring constantly, until thickened. Serve pot-roast with beans. (Serves 6 to 8)

Hot Chicken Chili

Norma Rowland -- Lafayette, Colorado

About 18 CHICKEN WINGS
FLOUR
OIL for frying
2 cans (16-oz.) KIDNEY BEANS
1 quart TOMATOES
SALT and PEPPER to taste
2 or 3 chopped JALAPENOS
1 small ONION (chopped)
2 or 3 cups WATER

Roll chicken wings in flour and fry in hot oil until crisp. Transfer to serving platter. Remove seeds from jalapeno peppers and chop. Combine jalapenos, kidney beans (drained), and remaining ingredients in skillet where wings were fried (don't throw grease away). Heat thoroughly, pour over wings and serve. Wings can be eaten with fingers. (Serves 4)

Tamale Pie

1 lb. GROUND BEEF
1 ONION (chopped)
1 tsp. GARLIC SALT
1 tsp. CHILI POWDER
SALT and PEPPER to taste
2 cans (7-oz.) TOMATO SAUCE
1 can (16-oz.) TOMATOES
1 can (16-oz.) BLACK OLIVES (chopped)
1 cup cooked RICE
1 can (16-oz.) CORN
¾ cup CORN MEAL
LONGHORN CHEESE (grated)

Brown hamburger with onion, salt, pepper, chili powder, and garlic salt. Drain, add remaining ingredients. Stir well to mix ingredients and bake at 350 F for 45 minutes to one hour. Grate cheese and sprinkle on top during last few minutes of baking, until melted. (Serves 6)

Tamale Loaf

1 cup CORN MEAL
4 cups WATER
1 lb. GROUND BEEF
1 med. ONION (chopped fine)
1 fresh GREEN PEPPER (chopped fine)
PARSLEY (minced)

1 clove GARLIC (minced)
2 Tbsp. FAT
1 can (16-oz.) TOMATOES
1 pint BLACK OLIVES
1 Tbsp. CHILI POWDER
SALT and PEPPER to taste

Make a mush of corn meal, salt and water. Brown meat, onion, pepper, parsley and garlic in fat. Add remaining ingredients. Combine mush and meat mixture and place in a casserole. Bake in a 400 F oven for 30 minutes.

Green Chile Egg Scramble

6 EGGS
½ tsp. SALT
6 to 12 GREEN CHILES (peeled, seeded, chopped fine)
2 tsp. FAT

Beat eggs slightly until yolks and whites are broken (but not too well mixed). Add chiles and salt. Heat fat in skillet until hot, but not smoking. Add egg mixture. Reduce heat and cook slowly, stirring the eggs from the bottom as they become firm. Serve when eggs are at desired firmness. (Serves 2)

Chiles Rellenos (Stuffed Chiles)

12 lg. CHILES (with stems)
1 lb. CHEESE
1 small ONION (chopped)

Peel chiles, but do not remove stems. Cut small slit length-wise below stem and remove veins and seeds. (Canned or frozen chiles may be used.) Combine cheese (grated, cubed or cut in strips) and onion. Stuff each chile carefully, to avoid breaking.

To coat chiles, dip stuffed chiles into one of the following batters and fry in deep fat until golden brown (turning once). Remove from fat and serve covered with heated sauce.

Batter #1 4 EGGS (separated)
¾ tsp. BAKING POWDER
4 Tbsp. FLOUR
¼ tsp. SALT

Beat egg whites until stiff. Beat yolks until thick. Sift together dry ingredients and add to yolks, blending well. Fold beaten whites into yolk mixture.

Batter #2 4 EGGS (separated)
½ tsp. SALT

Beat whites until fluffy. Beat in yolks and add salt.

Batter #3 1 cup FLOUR
1 tsp. BAKING POWDER
1 cup MILK
2 EGGS (slightly beaten)
½ tsp. SALT

Sift together dry ingredients. Combine eggs and milk. Add to flour mixture, stirring enough to mix.

Sauce for Chiles Rellenos

2 Tbsp. FAT
2 ONIONS (chopped)
3 cloves GARLIC
2 Tbsp. FLOUR
1 can (8-oz.) TOMATO PASTE
½ cup WATER
½ tsp. SALT

Heat fat and saute onions and garlic until golden brown. Add flour to heated fat and mix. Add remaining ingredients and cook to gravy consistency (at least 15 minutes).

TO BAKE CHILES: coat chiles, fry, drain, place in greased ovenproof dish, cover with sauce and top with grated cheese. Bake in 325 F oven until cheese melts (about 15 minutes).

Chiles Rellenos Casserole

Mrs. Robert H. Parker -- Phoenix, Arizona

1 lb. GROUND ROUND
½ cup ONION (chopped)
2 cans (4-oz.) GREEN CHILIS (diced)
SALT and PEPPER to taste
1½ cups CHEDDAR (grated)
1½ cups MILK
½ cup FLOUR
4 EGGS (beaten)

Brown meat and onion; drain fat; season to taste with salt and pepper. Spread half of chiles in 7x10'' baking dish. Sprinkle with cheese; top with meat mixture.

Combine milk and flour; mix well. Add to beaten eggs and pour over meat with remaining half of chiles. Bake in a 350 F oven for 45 to 50 minutes (or until knife inserted in center comes out clean). Serves 8

Dorothy's Chile Verde

Dorothy R. Smith -- Tucson, Arizona

1 Tbsp. SHORTENING
2 lbs. Boneless BEEF (1" cubes)
1 lg. (or 2 small) cloves GARLIC
   (minced)
2 cans (28-oz.) whole TOMATOES
1 cup (7-0z. can) GREEN CHILES
   (diced)
1 tsp. ground CUMIN
1/8 tsp. CHILE TEPINES
2 cups BEEF BROTH
SALT to taste

Melt shortening in a large pot with a lid. Add meat slowly and brown. Add garlic during last five minutes of browning and cook until soft. Add liquid from tomatoes. Chop and add the tomatoes. Stir in remaining ingredients EXCEPT salt. Bring mixture to a boil and cover. Reduce heat and simmer about two hours. Stir occasionally. When meat is very tender, taste and add salt. (Lid may be removed for additional 30 munutes cooking time if sauce is too thin.) (Serves 6)

Chiles Relleno Bake

Courtesy Ashley's of Texas

2 cans or jars (4-oz.) Ashley's
  Whole GREEN CHILES
3 cups Monterey Jack CHEESE
  (grated)
1 cup sharp Cheddar CHEESE
  (grated)
2 EGGS (beaten)
1 Tbsp. FLOUR
2 Tbsp. MILK

Cut chiles in thin strips. Layer chiles and cheeses in an oiled 9" baking dish. Combine eggs, flour and milk. Pour over chiles and cheese. Bake in 375 F oven for 50 minutes (or until firm). Cool five minutes and cut in squares. (Serves 6)

Spanish Pie

Dr. Mercedes Hoskins -- Las Cruces, N. M. (Courtesy ICGRC)

1 cup BACON PIECES
1 cup BACON DRIPPINGS
2 cups CORN MEAL
1 tsp. SODA
1 tsp. SALT
1½ cups MILK
4 EGGS
2 cans (16-oz.) Cream Style CORN
½ cup BELL PEPPER (chopped)
1 cup GREEN CHILE (chopped)
½ cup PIMENTOS (chopped)
2 cups CHEDDAR (grated)

Fry crisp enough bacon to make one cup pieces and one cup drippings.

Sift cornmeal, soda, and salt together; add milk, eggs and 2/3 cup bacon drippings. Stir in corn, bell pepper, pimento, and bacon pieces. Oil a 9x15 pan (or two square 9-inch pans) with remaining drippings. Pour in half of batter and layer with chiles and 1 1/2 cups cheese. Add remaining batter. Bake in a 400 F oven for 25 minutes. Sprinkle with remaining cheese and bake 10 minutes more. Cool slightly before serving. (Serves 6 to 8)

Mom's Chili Stew

Ellie Cook -- Saugus, California

1¾ lbs. GROUND ROUND
1 small ONION (chopped)
1 Tbsp. CHILI POWDER
1 tsp. Lawry's Seasoned SALT
1/8 tsp. PEPPER
1 can (28-oz.) whole TOMATOES
1 stalk CELERY
4 CARROTS
1 can TOMATO SOUP (undiluted)
2 cans (16-oz.) KIDNEY BEANS

Brown ground round with onions. Season with 1/2 tablespoon chili powder, 1/2 teaspoon Lawry's Seasoned Salt and 1/16 teaspoon pepper. Mash tomatoes and add to meat. Dice celery and carrots and add with tomato soup to meat. Simmer for 25 minutes. Then add kidney beans (with liquid) and remainder of seasonings. Simmer for one hour. (Serves 8 to 10)

Red Flannel Stew

2 Tbsp. Cooking FAT
1 lg. ONION (chopped)
2 cups cooked PINTO BEANS
1 can (12-oz.) CORNED BEEF
1 can (16-oz.) TOMATOES
½ lb. CHEDDAR (cubed)
CHILI POWDER to taste
Corn Tortillas

Brown onions in cooking fat. Add one cup cooked beans and mash into a paste.

Add remaining beans, meat, chile powder, and tomatoes. Heat thoroughly. Add cubes of cheese and heat to melt. Serve on fried tortillas. (Serves 6)

Mexican Casserole

3 cups cooked BEANS
1 cup canned TOMATOES
2 Tbsp. GREEN PEPPER (chopped)
GARLIC SALT
¾ cup ONION (chopped)
½ tsp. SALT
1 tsp. CHILE POWDER
4 strips BACON

Combine all ingredients, except bacon. Turn into greased baking dish. Arrange bacon strips over top. Bake in a 350 F oven for one hour. (Serves 4)

Fish Chili Hot Pot

Courtesy Gebhardt's Mexican Foods -- San Antonio, Texas

1 lb. RED KIDNEY BEANS
1½ quarts boiling WATER
1½ tsp. SALT
1 cup uncooked RICE
2 sliced, peeled ONIONS
2 sliced BELL PEPPERS
1 clove GARLIC (minced)
2 Tbsp. BUTTER
1 Tbsp. Gebhardt's CHILI POWDER
¼ tsp. PEPPER
1 can (6-oz.) TOMATO PASTE
1 lb. FISH FILLETS (any kind)

Pour boiling water over beans. Add the salt. Cover and let stand 50 minutes. Then boil for 1 1/4 hours. Add the rice, and cook together until both are almost tender, about 20 minutes.

Meantime, saute the onions, green peppers and garlic in the margarine until they turn color. Stir into the bean and rice mixture. Then add the chili powder and pepper, and the tomato paste mixed with an equal amount of water. Simmer 10 minutes. Then cut fish in 1/2 inch cubes and add. Simmer 20 minutes and serve very hot. (Serves 4 to 6)

Stuffed Fish

2 lbs. HALIBUT
2 Tbsp. FAT
1 small ONION (chopped)
2 cloves GARLIC (chopped)
3 TOMATOES (chopped)
½ cup GREEN CHILE (chopped)
3 EGGS (beaten)
1 cup ALMONDS (chopped)
1 tsp. PARSLEY (chopped)
SALT to taste

Clean fish and remove bones. Saute onion and garlic in hot fat; add chopped tomatoes. Stir in egg and cook until eggs curdle. Add nuts, parsley, chile and salt. Stuff fish with mixture; place in cheesecloth and tie shut. Bake in a greased baking dish in a 350 F oven about one hour. (Serves 4 to 6)

Ceviche

1½ lbs. FISH FILLETS (raw)
1 cup fresh LEMON JUICE
2 canned GREEN CHILES (chopped)
½ cup ONION (chopped
2 fresh TOMATOES
1 tsp. SALT
¼ tsp. OREGANO
¼ cup OLIVE OIL
Chopped CILANTRO
AVOCADO slices

Cut fish fillets into small, thin pieces. Cover with lemon juice and refrigerate (covered) for two hours. Peel, seed and cut tomatoes into pieces. Combine fish with tomatoes and other ingredients, stir, and serve icy cold. Garnish with slices of avocado, chopped parsley, cilantro, etc.

Chile and Mushroom Omelet

Yolanda Alexander -- Las Cruces, N. M. (Courtesy ICGRC)

Omelet

2 EGGS
1 Tbsp. CREAM
Dash of SALT
1 Tbsp. BUTTER

For each omelet, you will need 2 eggs, 1 tablespoon cream, 1 tablespoon butter, and a dash of salt. Mix eggs, cream, and salt well, preferably with wire whisk.

Melt butter in omelet pan until golden-brown. Add eggs, scrambling just enough so all the egg gets cooked. When omelet is shiny and just moist on top, remove from heat and spoon on 1/2 cup filling; top with 1 tablespoon grated cheese. Fold omelet in half and flip onto serving plate. Prepare additional omelets in the same way.

Filling

BUTTER
½ cup GREEN CHILES (chopped)
4 med. Fresh MUSHROOMS (sliced)
1 small ONION (sliced thin)
½ lb. Canadian BACON (chopped)
½ lb. sharp CHEDDAR (grated)

Melt butter in medium-sized pan. Add all ingredients EXCEPT cheese, and saute until onions are limp and mushrooms are tender.

Rice Tortes with Shredded Shrimp

Antonio G. Castro -- Phoenix, Arizona

2 cups Long Grain RICE
5 EGGS
1 pkg. Shredded Dry SHRIMP
½ lb. LARD
1 fresh TOMATO (diced)
½ White ONION (diced)
3 GREEN ONIONS (chopped)
3 GREEN CHILE PEPPERS
  (roasted and peeled)
Chopped CELERY (small amount)
1 can (48-oz.) V-8
1 sm. bunch fresh CILANTRO
  (chopped)
SALT and PEPPER to taste
2 to 3 cups WATER
5 Chicken BOUILLON CUBES

Soak rice about 15 to 30 minutes. Blend rice in blender on slow speed 10 seconds (or until rice is broken into small pieces). Take rice out of blender and put into medium bowl. Add eggs and shrimp. Mix well.

Next, heat lard in a large skillet. Take two full tablespoons of shrimp mixture and drop into hot lard, to make torte. Fry both sides of torte well. Set aside while preparing vegetables. Fry tomatoes, onions, celery, green chiles in some lard about one minute. Next, add remaining ingredients, and let boil for a few minutes. Add tortes and cook for another 30 minutes over low fire. (Serves 6)

Veal with Chile

1½ lb. VEAL STEAK
3 Tbsp. FLOUR
1 Tbsp. CHILE POWDER
½ tsp. SALT
4 Tbsp. OLIVE OIL (or cooking oil)
1 med. ONION (minced)
1 cup SOUR CREAM
1 clove GARLIC (mashed)

Cut veal into serving portions. Combine flour, chile powder and salt to dredge meat. Brown meat in hot oil. Add remaining ingredients. Cover and bake in 325 F oven for one hour (or until meat is tender). (Serves 4)

Green Enchiladas

1 cup GREEN CHILES (chopped)
1 Tbsp. FAT
1 med. ONION (chopped)
SALT to taste
1 cup canned TOMATOES (drained)
½ cup SWEET CREAM (or evaporated milk)
6 CORN TORTILLAS
1 cup CHEDDAR CHEESE (grated)

Roast and peel green chiles. Remove stem, seeds, and veins (or use canned or frozen chile) and chop fine. Saute onion in fat. Add tomatoes and chopped chile.

Gradually add cream, stirring constantly. Simmer five minutes.

Fry tortillas in about 1/2 inch of fat in a heavy skillet, turning once, cooking about 1/2 minute for each side.

Arrange on hot serving plate in layers--tortilla, sauce, cheese, then repeat. Keep in warm oven until ready to serve. (Serves 2)

Confetti Chicken Chile Rellenos

Nancy Keddy -- Los Alamos, New Mexico

18 to 20 whole GREEN CHILES
1 cup cooked CHICKEN (chopped)
2 cups Monterey JACK CHEESE
(grated)
¼ cup ONION (chopped)
3 EGGS (separated)
1 Tbsp. WATER
3 Tbsp. FLOUR
¼ tsp. SALT
½ pint SOUR CREAM
2 Tbsp. PIMENTO (chopped)
1 Tbsp. CHIVES (chopped)

Filling: Combine chicken, cheese and onion. Pat chiles dry on paper towels and stuff with chicken mixture.

Batter: Beat egg yolks with water, flour and salt; fold into beaten egg whites and set aside.

Topping: Combine sour cream, pimento and chives.

Dip stuffed chiles into flour and then egg batter. Fry in hot oil (1" to 1 1/2" deep) turning once, until golden. Drain on paper towels. Top with mound of confetti topping. (Serves 6)

Cowboy Green Chili Beef Bake

Gracie McCormack -- Phoenix, Arizona
(Courtesy American National Cowbelles)

2½ lbs. Beef ROUND STEAK
2 Tbsp. COOKING FAT
1 Tbsp. Dehydr. ONION
½ tsp. CHILI POWDER (optional)
¼ tsp. OREGANO
SALT to taste

¼ tsp. GARLIC (minced)
1 small bunch GREEN ONIONS
1 can (4-oz.) chopped
  GREEN CHILES
1 can (4½-oz.) RIPE OLIVES
  (chopped)
1 Tbsp. CORNSTARCH mixed
  with ¼ cup hot water
1 pkg. (8) Refrig. CRESCENT
  ROLLS
2 cans (15-oz.) PINTO BEANS
2 cans (10-oz.) TOMATOES and
  GREEN CHILES
10 to 16 oz. Sharp CHEDDAR
  (shredded)
PARSLEY (optional)

Cut green onions into 1" pieces. Drain green chiles and pinto beans.

Remove bone and fat from steak; slice into bite-size pieces. Heat fat in 10" skillet and add meat, onion, chili powder, oregano, salt, garlic, green onions, chiles and olives. Cook until meat is browned. Add cornstarch mixture to meat and simmer until thickened, stirring occasionally.

Place crescent rolls on lightly greased cookie sheet. Put small amount of meat mixture on each roll, and roll according to package directions. Cover with wax paper and set aside.

In a lightly-greased 2 1/2 quart casserole, put one can pinto beans (drained); add one can tomatoes and green chiles on top. Place a layer of 1/2 of remaining meat mixture in casserole and top with 1/2 the cheese.. Repeat the four layers. Bake in a 325 F oven for 15 minutes. Place crescent rolls in oven. Continue baking casserole and rolls for 20 minutes more. Remove from oven; arrange rolls on casserole; garnish. (Serves 8)

Green Chile Souffle

1 can (3-oz.) EVAPORATED MILK
3 EGGS
½ tsp. SALT
½ lb. CHEDDAR (grated)
9 to 12 peeled GREEN CHILES

Combine all ingredients in blender until chiles are chopped. Pour mixture into buttered baking dish and bake in 350 oven for 1/2 hour. (Serves 4)

Peppy Pecan Balls

Jimmy Lou Buescher -- Las Cruces, N. M. (Courtesy ICGRC)

> 1 pkg. (8-oz.) CREAM CHEESE
> ¾ lb. sharp CHEDDAR (grated fine)
> 2 cans (4-oz.) GREEN CHILE (chopped & drained)
> 1 cup ground PECANS

Combine grated Cheddar and softened cream cheese, mixing well. Stir in green chiles and mix thoroughly. Form into bite-size balls and roll in pecans. Chill until firm.

Chile Cheese Balls

Eleanor G. Wootten -- Shawnee Mission, Kan. (Courtesy ICGRC)

> 2 cups sharp CHEDDAR (grated)
> ½ cup soft MARGARINE
> 1 cup FLOUR
> ½ tsp. SALT
> 1 can (4-oz.) GREEN CHILES (chopped)

Stir together creamed margarine, cheese, flour, and salt. Add chopped green chiles and mix well. Form dough into 3/4-inch balls. Bake in pre-heated 375 F oven for 12 to 15 minutes. Serve warm. Balls can be made in advance and frozen. Bake frozen balls about 18 minutes.

Chile Cheese Sticks

Phyllis Selders -- Las Cruces, N. M. (Courtesy ICGRC)

> ¾ cup FLOUR (sifted)
> ½ tsp. SALT
> ¼ cup SHORTENING
> 1/3 cup CHEESE (grated)
> 3 Tbsp. GREEN CHILE & Juice (chopped)
> 1 EGG WHITE (slightly beaten)
> COARSE SALT

Drain chiles and reserve liquid. Sift flour and salt; cut in shortening. Stir in chiles and cheese. Sprinkle mixture with reserved juice, adding water if necessary to make enough liquid to moisten flour so dough can be pressed into ball. Roll out dough to thin sheet (1/4'' thick). Cut into 1/2x4'' strips. Brush with egg white and sprinkle with coarse salt. Bake on lightly greased cookie sheet in 425 F oven about 12 minutes (until lightly brown).

Corn Pie

½ lb. BUTTER
1 cup SUGAR
4 EGGS
1 can (4-oz.) chopped
   GREEN CHILES
1 can (16-oz.) Cream Style
   CORN
½ cup JACK CHEESE (shredded)
½ cup mild CHEDDAR (shredded)
1 cup FLOUR
1 cup Yellow CORNMEAL
4 tsp. BAKING POWDER
¼ tsp. SALT

Preheat oven to 350 F. Cream butter and sugar. Add eggs, one at a time, mixing well. Add chile, corn and cheese and mix well.

Sift flour and then measure. Sift cornmeal and then measure. Sift flour and cornmeal together with baking powder and salt; add to corn mixture, blending well. Pour into greased and floured 8x12x2 baking dish. Reduce oven heat to 300 F and bake one hour. (Serves 10)

Chili Turnovers

Courtesy The Quaker Oats Company -- Chicago, Illinois

Masa Pastry

¾ cup Quaker MASA HARINA
½ cup sifted All-Purpose FLOUR
2 tsp. BAKING POWDER
2 Tbsp. SHORTENING (liquid or
   melted)
½ cup warm WATER

Filling

1¼ cups (10½-oz. can) CHILI

For Masa pastry, sift together Masa Harina, flour and baking powder. Add shortening and water and stir until blended. Knead dough with hands about 1/2 minute. Divide dough into six parts. Shape each to form a ball. Roll each ball between two sheets of waxed paper to form a circle (about 7" across). Remove top sheet of waxed paper.

Place about 3 tablespoons chili on half of circle; fold other half of dough over top. Peel back waxed paper. Press edges of Masa pastry to seal; flute edges. Prick top with fork. Invert turnover on hand; peel off waxed paper and place on lightly-greased cookie sheet. Bake in preheated hot oven (400 F) about 20 minutes. (Makes 6)

Red Chile Apple Pie

5 cups APPLES (peeled and sliced)
¾ cup SUGAR
2 Tbsp. BUTTER
1 tsp. CINNAMON
½ tsp. NUTMEG
2 tsp. CHILE POWDER
1 cup WATER
DASH of SALT

Combine all ingredients in large saucepan and cook over medium heat about 20 to 25 minutes. Pour into 9" unbaked pie shell, dot with butter. Top with crust, cut vents and sprinkle with sugar. Bake 30 to 40 minutes in 375 F oven (or until crust is brown).

Green Chile Pinwheels

2 cups CHEDDAR (grated)
1 cup FLOUR
½ tsp. SALT
¼ lb. BUTTER (melted)
1 can (8-oz.) GREEN CHILE (chopped)

Mix first three ingredients together, then add the butter and knead until thoroughly blended. Roll out in a rectangular shape until approximately 1/8" thick. Spread with chopped green chile and roll up like a jelly roll. Chill. Slice the same as for refrigerator cookies. Bake in 350 F oven for approximately 10 minutes.

Chile and Cheese Pancake

7 to 12 fresh GREEN CHILES
1 EGG (separated)
1½ tsp. FLOUR
½ tsp. OREGANO
SALT to taste

½ cup CHEDDAR (grated)
¼ cup CELERY (chopped)
1/3 cup ONION (chopped)
½ tsp. Worcestershire Sauce

Peel chiles; remove stems, seeds, and veins and chop fine. (To substitute for fresh chiles, use 1/2 cup frozen or canned chopped chile.)

Beat egg white until stiff. Beat egg yolk and add flour, oregano, and salt. Mix well, add to egg white, then fold in remaining ingredients. Drop small amounts on a slightly greased griddle, brown on both sides, reduce heat, and finish cooking.

Chili 'n Cheese Cups

Courtesy The Quaker Oats Company -- Chicago, Illinois

Masa Cups

1 cup Quaker MASA HARINA
1 Tbsp. SHORTENING
(liquid or melted)
¼ cup warm WATER
¼ tsp. SALT

Filling

¾ cup CHILI
12 small Cheddar Cheese
Slices (1¼" square)

For cups, mix all ingredients thoroughly. Divide and shape into 12 balls. Place each ball in a greased muffin cup. Press Masa mixture evenly on sides and bottom of each muffin cup. Place 1 tablespoon chili in each Masa-lined cup. Bake in preheated oven (400 F) 20 minutes. Top each chili cup with one square of cheese. Bake about 5 additional minutes. Let stand a few minutes, then remove from muffin cups. (Serves 12)

Chile-Egg Squares

Carrie Knauth -- Albuquerque, N.M. (Courtesy ICGRC)

2 cans (4-oz.) GREEN CHILES (chopped)
2 cups CHEDDAR (coarsely grated)
8 EGGS (slightly beaten)
8 Tbsp. CREAM
SALT and PEPPER to taste

Spread chopped chiles in bottom of greased 9x13 cake pan. Cover chiles with grated cheese. Combine eggs, cream, and seasonings and pour over cheese layer. Bake in 350 F oven for 30 minutes. Cool in pan for several minutes. Cut into bars and serve.

Pickled Jalapeños

JALAPEÑO PEPPERS
VINEGAR
OLIVE OIL
SALT
PICKLING SPICES

Wash jalapeño peppers and pack tightly in quart jars. For every cup of vinegar, use 1/4 cup olive oil, one teaspoon salt and one teaspoon pickling spices. Heat mixture to boil. Pour over peppers so they are well-covered, leaving one-inch head space. Seal jars and process 10 minutes in hot water bath.

Chile Jelly

Mrs. Robert Strain -- Rio Rancho, N. M. (Courtesy ICGRC)

4 whole GREEN CHILES (peeled & seeded)
4 lg. BELL PEPPERS
1 cup VINEGAR
5½ cups SUGAR
1 bottle (6-oz.) LIQUID FRUIT PECTIN

Wash and remove core and seeds from bell peppers and drain chiles. Dice bell pepper and grind with chiles in food chopper. Add vinegar and sugar and boil until mixture is transparent, about 1/2 hour. Remove from heat and let cool for 5 to 10 minutes. Add liquid fruit pectin and stir well. Pour jelly into 1/2 pint jars and seal.

Hot Pepper Jelly #1

Mrs. Robert H. Parker -- Phoenix, Arizona

¾ cup CHILI PEPPERS
1 med. BELL PEPPER
1¼ cups VINEGAR
6 cups SUGAR
3 drops Green FOOD COLOR
6 oz. CERTO

Skin, seed and chop enough peppers to fill 3/4 cup. Seed and chop one green bell pepper. Combine chili peppers and bell pepper with vinegar in a blender and blend. Add blended liquid to sugar in a large saucepan. Bring to a rolling boil and add food coloring. Skim and add Certo; boil two minutes, stirring constantly. Then cool five minutes, stirring constantly. Pour into sterilized jars, seal with paraffin. (Makes six 8-oz. jars)

Hot Pepper Jelly #2

Mrs. Robert H. Parker -- Phoenix, Arizona

6 lg. Hot RED PEPPERS
1 LEMON
VINEGAR
1½ cups SUGAR

Skin and seed peppers and put through food chopper. Quarter and seed lemon (leave skin on). Cover peppers with cold water and bring to a boiling point. Boil for five minutes. Drain thoroughly. Add lemon quarters and enough vinegar to cover. Cook 30 minutes, then add sugar. Boil 10 minutes. Remove lemon. Pour into sterilized jars, seal with paraffin. (Makes four 6-oz. jars.)

Green Chile Wine

Sam Arnold -- Denver, Colorado

1 lb. GREEN CHILES (peeled and seeds removed)
3 lbs. SUGAR
1 gallon WATER
¼ tsp. GRAPE TANNIN
1 BISULFITE TABLET
3 YEAST NUTRIENT TABLETS
1 oz. ACID BLEND
24 DRIED APRICOT HALVES
½ cup RAISINS (coarsely chopped)
1 packet All-Purpose WINE YEAST

Chop green chiles into 1/4" squares. Dissolve sugar in very warm water. Crush bisulfite and yeast tablets into a powder. Mix together all ingredients EXCEPT wine yeast in five-gallon polythene bucket. Cover with plastic wrap. (This mixture is called the MUST.) When must has cooled to 70-75 degrees, sprinkle yeast on top. Cover bucket. Stir must daily. Ferment for five days.

Strain out solids and press leftover pulp. Discard pulp. Siphon must into narrow-necked one-gallon jug or carboy. Cover with double layer of plastic wrap secured with rubber band or attached fermentation lock. Be sure liquid is topped by adding water to bring level within 1" of top of jug. Place jug away from drafts or extreme temperature changes. After three weeks, siphon wine into 5-gallon bucket, leaving as much of the yeast deposit behind as possible. Carefully rinse jug and siphon wine back into jug. Top liquid again. Replace cover. (This process is called RACKING.) After three months repeat the racking process.

When wine is clear and bubbles can no longer be seen rising in the liquid, bottle the wine. If corks are used, store bottles on their sides. If screw caps, store upright. Age one year.

Chile Cheese Puffs

Mrs. Robert H. Parker -- Phoenix, Arizona

1 tsp. BUTTER
1½ tsp. FLOUR
1 cup SKIM MILK
¼ lb. CHEDDAR (grated)
1 can (4-oz.) GREEN CHILES (chopped)

½ tsp. SALT
Dash PEPPER
1 EGG (separated)
2 doz. TOAST ROUNDS

Melt butter and add flour, blending well. Gradually add milk and cook until thickened. Add cheese and stir until melted. Add chiles and season. Beat egg yolk and add. Fold in stiffly beaten egg white. Pile on toast rounds and put under broiler until puffed and lightly brown. (Serves 24)

Jalapeño Cornbread

Mrs. Daniel K. White -- Cameron, Missouri

3 cups CORNBREAD MIX
(yellow)
2½ cups MILK
½ cup CORN OIL
3 EGGS (beaten)
1 lg. ONION (diced)
½ tsp. GARLIC SALT
3 tsp. SUGAR
1 can (17-oz.) Creamed CORN
½ cup JALAPEÑO PEPPERS
(chopped)
1½ cups CHEDDAR (grated)

Seed jalapeño peppers and chop. Combine with other ingredients and mix well. Bake in greased 9x12x2 baking pan in 400 F oven for one hour (or until done in middle).

Chile Bread

Mrs.Corann M. Pesqueira -- Las Cruces,N.M. (Courtesy ICGRC)

1 cup YELLOW CORNMEAL
1 tsp. BAKING POWDER
1 tsp. SALT
½ tsp. BAKING SODA
1 cup BUTTERMILK
2 Tbsp. BUTTER (melted)
2 EGGS (beaten)
1 can (8-oz.) Cream-Style CORN
1 ONION (chopped)
1 can (4-oz.) GREEN CHILE (chopped)
1 cup LONGHORN CHEESE (grated)

Mix cornmeal, salt, soda, and baking powder. Stir in the remaining ingredients, mixing well. Pour into greased loaf pan. Bake in 350 F oven for 45 minutes. Cool for 10 minutes, slice and serve.

Chile Copita

2 shots TEQUILA
6-oz. Snappy Tom or Bloody Mary Mix
1 whole GREEN CHILE POD (canned)

Place all ingredients in blender and liquefy. Serve over ice. (Chile Copita is the official drink of International Connoisseurs of Green & Red Chile.)

Freezing Green Chile

Mae Martha Johnson, Extension Foods and Nutrition Specialist,
Cooperative Extension Service of New Mexico State University

Green chile is a good source of vitamins A and C. Frozen at the peak of summer goodness, this delicious vegetable can add nutrition and variety to meals.

Selection

Choose chile that is mature, heavy for its size, smooth and symmetrical, bright green in color, fresh, and crisp.

Avoid misshapen pods, shriveled skin, mold, soft spots, and bruises.

Blistering

The tough outer skin must be removed from the chile. Blistering the skin by one of the following methods makes removal easy. The skin may then be removed before or after freezing.

Handling pungent chile can burn hands and eyes. Protect hands with a thin layer of solid fat or by wearing rubber gloves. Keep hands away from eyes while working with chile.

Wash and dry chile. With a knife, make a small slit in the side to allow steam to escape. Be sure heat source is very hot. Turn frequently to prevent scorching and insure even blistering. Remove from heat and spread out on a flat surface in a single layer to cool before peeling. For a more crisp product, dip chile into ice water as it is removed from heat. For more thoroughly-cooked chile, place in a pan and cover with a damp towel for a few minutes.

The following are three heat-source methods for blistering chile:

Oven or broiler method—Place chiles in a hot oven or broiler 400° to 450°F (205° to 232°C), for six to eight minutes until skin blisters so that it can be pulled away from the flesh.

Range top method—Place chiles on a hot electric

Blistering (cont'd)

or gas burner after covering burner with a layer of heavy wire mesh.

Outdoor grill method—Place chiles on a charcoal grill about five to six inches above glowing coals.

Peeling After Blistering

Removal of the outer skin is easier after freezing. If freezer space permits, cooled, blistered chiles may be packed and frozen.

As the chile is peeled, before or after freezing, slit along the sides and remove seeds and veins. Stems may be left attached for chiles rellenos.

Packaging

Pack whole unpeeled chiles in plastic bags or wrap in heavy aluminum foil or freezer wrap. Press down to remove all air and seal.

Peeled chiles, whole or diced, can be packaged in plastic bags or rigid containers of glass, metal, or plastic. Leave one-half inch head space. Seal.

Freezing and Storage

Freeze chiles immediately after packing. Freeze at $0^\circ F$ $(-18^\circ C)$ or below. Put no more food into the home freezer than will freeze within 24 hours. Usually this is about two or three pounds of food to each cubic foot of freezer capacity. For quickest freezing, place packages against freezing plates or coils and leave a little space between packages so air can circulate freely.

After freezing, packages may be stored close together. Store them at $0^\circ F$, $(-18^\circ C)$, or below.

Why are chile peppers hot?

The heat is generated by a substance in the interior ribs or strings of the chiles, rather than in the seeds. Since the seeds are in such proximity with the veins, they carry the essence of hotness. In general, the smaller the pepper, the more potent its "bite," though some varieties have strains which vary in their degree of heat. Peppers which are harvested have often reached their maximum degree of hotness; peppers left on the vine to dry become somewhat sweeter, rather than hotter.

Canning Chile Sauces

Mae Martha Johnson, Extension Foods and Nutrition Specialist, Cooperative Extension Service of New Mexico State University

Green chile sauces are commonly found on the table in southwestern homes. Chile, by itself, is a low-acid vegetable, which must be pressure-canned to be safe. Most chile sauces are a combination of green chile and tomatoes.

If sufficient vinegar is added, these sauces can be preserved by methods suitable for canning high-acid vegetables and fruits.

Since many homes do not have pressure-canning equipment, the following recipes were developed for the water-bath method.

Green Chile and Tomatoes

3 cups tomatoes, peeled and chopped
3 cups green chile, peeled and chopped (seeds removed if desired)
1½ teaspoons salt
1¼ cups vinegar

Taco Sauce with Green Chile

3 cups tomatoes, peeled and chopped
3 cups green chile, peeled and chopped (seeds removed if desired)
¾ cup onion, chopped
1½ teaspoons salt
3 garlic cloves, minced
1½ cups vinegar

Taco Sauce with Jalapeño

3 cups tomatoes, peeled and chopped
3 cups jalapeño, seeded and finely chopped
¾ cup onion, chopped
1½ teaspoon salt
3 garlic cloves, minced
1½ cups vinegar

Prepare each of the above recipes as follows:

Combine all ingredients, bring to a boil, cover, and simmer five minutes. Pack in hot, clean jars. *Use all the liquid. Divide it evenly among the jars.* Adjust lids. Process in water-bath for 30 minutes. Start counting processing time when water returns to boiling. Yield: About 4 pints or 8 half pints per recipe.

Water Bath Canning

A water-bath canner or any big metal container may be used, if it is deep enough so that the water is well over tops of jars and has space to boil freely. Allow 2 to 4 inches above jar tops. The canner must have a tight-fitting cover and a wire or wooden rack. If the rack has dividers, jars will not touch each other or fall against the sides of the canner during processing.

Add boiling water if needed to bring the water an inch or two over tops of containers; don't pour boiling water directly on glass jars. Put cover on canner. Add boiling water during processing if needed to keep containers covered.

Remove containers from the canner immediately when processing time is up. Do not disturb seal.

At an altitude of 1,000 feet or more, you have to add to the processing time in canning directions, as follows:

Altitude	Add
3,000 feet	6 minutes
4,000 feet	8 minutes
5,000 feet	10 minutes
6,000 feet	12 minutes
7,000 feet	14 minutes
8,000 feet	16 minutes
9,000 feet	18 minutes

Notes
- An equal amount of lemon juice may be used to replace all or part of the vinegar.
- The recipes may be altered by using less chile, but not by using more chile.
- Additional seasonings such as oregano, cilantro, etc. will be better if added when served rather than before canning.
- More salt may be added if desired.
- If a less acid sauce is desired, it should be pressure canned or frozen.

Funding for the development of these canning recipes was provided by the International Connoisseurs of Red and Green Chile; consultants were Dr. Ricardo Gomez, Extension Horticulturist, and Shirley Jaquez. The Departments of Home Economics and Horticulture provided use of facilities.

Supply Sources

Hayden Flour Mills
119 Mill Ave.,
Tempe, AZ 85281
   (Rose Brand Pinto Beans)

Lawry's Foods, Inc.
570 W. Avenue 26
Los Angeles, CA 90065
   (Lawry's Texas Style
     Chili Seasoning Mix)

Sam Lewis & Associates
704 First Savings Bldg.
San Angelo, TX 76901
   (Jalapeño Lollipops)

McIlhenny Company
Avery Island
New Orleans, LA 70513
   (Tabasco Brand Pepper Sauce)

Reily Food Co.
640 Magazine St.
New Orleans, LA 70130
(Wick Fowler's 2-Alarm Chili)
(Carroll Shelby's Texas Chili)

Santa Cruz Chili & Spice Co.
P. O. Box 177
Tumacacori, AZ 85640
   (Chili paste and chile products)

Index